GHOST STORIES

of Berks County, PA.

by Charles J. Adams III

ON THE COVER

This "old haunted house" of Vinemont, South Heidelberg Township, was demolished in 1970, but the magnificently eerie building looms in the memories of anyone who savored the spook stories of South Mountain. The building was erected around an original log structure built sometime near 1800. The classic photograph was taken by Reading EAGLE-TIMES photographer J. Charles Gardner, for a March 21, 1970 TIMES article in which noted writer and local personality Ray Koehler described the former Hertzel Mansion as looking like "a honeymoon cottage for ghouls."

GHOST STORIES
of Berks County
Copyright (c) 1982 by Charles J. Adams III
Published by the author
ISBN: 0-9610008-0-5

Printed in the U.S.A.

FOREWORD

Throughout this book you will notice that many, if not all of the names of those involved have been either changed or omitted. This is by design. Furthermore, even when names are used, it can be assumed that they are not those of the actual person involved in the story. The exceptions are those individuals of historical importance or names which have already appeared in other published acounts. The author is grateful to those Berks Countians who gave their time and confidence during the exhaustive research for this volume. To assure their anonymity and protect their privacy, this method has been employed.

In each case, the identity of these individuals is recorded and documented in the notes and files of the author. While the credibility of the stories may suffer a bit, they remain a collection of simply that — stories.

The time-honored diversion of "telling ghost stories," be it around a crackling camp fire or on a rainy night inside a quiet house is one of the true pleasures of life. And it is probable that many of the enduring ghost stories of the last century may have had their beginnings in the realm of entertainment, in days when story-telling was an art. The simplicity of a ghost story, per se, has been enhanced, if that's the correct word, by modern psychic research and theory upon theory. But that is not the intent of this book. What you are about to read are ghost stories. Just stories. Stories told by Berks Countians a century ago, a half-century ago, today, and probably for many tomorrows.

PREFACE

Do ghosts exist?

This is one of the most common questions asked of this Berks County ghost hunter. The answer has to be, "of course ghosts exist!" To borrow a thought from the immortal holiday editorial, ghosts exist in the hearts and minds of those touched by them. These "ghosts" could merely be memories of departed loved ones brought to life, so to speak, by a spark of imagination and kindled by the love which knows no boundary as frail as death.

Or, ghosts could be absolute, undeniable inhabitants of the spirit world, the "other side," who make their existence known to the select and fortunate few who have been programmed in the great scheme of things to receive them freely. How can one dispute the story told by a Berks Countian of simple roots, whose brow moistens and lips quiver as their unexplainable tale is delivered in trembling voice? Why would any of these people give their time and whatever small part of their very personal experiences to a stranger seeking sensationalistic supernatural stories? These people have nothing to gain and in some cases much to lose by telling their tales, considered by many to be on the edge of lunacy.

It may be worth noting that the capcity of the human mind seems to be ever expanding. And its capacity to understand itself travels over new horizons of comprehension almost constantly. What was unheard of psychologically and psychically just decades ago is now commonly accepted. Technology, the mechanical manifestation of the mind, has aided in this acceptance.

The author's favorite and daringly rational explanation of ghostly occurrences is really quite simple, but does require some thought.

Technology has enabled man to record his voice and almost every sound around him on rust — ferrous oxide — the refined product we call recording tape. Through electrical impulses, these sounds are recorded permanently on rust. Imagine now, the electrical impulses of the human brain at the time of extreme trauma, such as a sudden death. Could not these electrical impulses, these "brain waves," which normally travel through the complex human nervous system be burst from the confines of the body and into the atmosphere around it? Could not these impulses in turn, be recorded much as on oxide tape on any waiting piece of ferrous oxide nearby?

One of the other questions most asked is if the ghost stories follow any particular pattern. In retrospect, it can be noted that many do indeed have their origins in old houses and even more specifically, remodeled old houses. In the process of this remodeling, architectural "ghosts," if you will, are unveiled. This is not to suggest that spirits may simply dwell inside walls and under floorboards, but what about the simple implements that help keep the walls and floorboards together?

Nails.

In some cases, rusty nails!

Again, could it not be possible that these electrical impulses emitted by the brain at a cataclysmic time could be "recorded" on the rust, and "played back" at a later time? Could it not be possible that a receptive mind such as that of a "medium," could receive these impulses? Could they not then be played back through the medium as a vivid account of the innermost secrets of the life and death of the victim?

These are bold propositions, perhaps, but a century ago, the idea of tape recording was just as incredible.

That ghosts do or do not exist is not the issue here. The purpose of this book is to compile, for whatever purpose, some of the experiences Berks Countians have had with the supernatural. I truly hope you enjoy the stories.

Charles J. Adams III
Reading, PA, 1982

TABLE OF CONTENTS

GHOST STORIES OF BERKS COUNTY

Introduction to the 1997 Second Edition
and the "lost conclusion" of
The Ghost on the Throne

by Charles J. Adams III

When the necessity to repackage the original "Ghost Stories of Berks County" came about in early 1997, it was also an opportunity to breathe new life into the cover and right a wrong which had festered within me for 15 years.

That first book on ghosts and legends in my native county was never intended to be the first of three ghost books in Berks and the start of an unimaginable journey through haunted places in four states.

Looking back after about 20 books and inestimable experiences in researching, writing, editing, and publishing, I still haven't gotten it right yet, but my partner and publisher Dave Seibold give it our best with every new book.

We've come a long way from typewriters to computers, cheapest-we-can-find print shops to one of the best in the business, and from the ghosts in Maidencreek to the ghosts in Manhattan.

When I made what I considered a daring decision to publish my own book back in 1982, I raided the family savings account, hacked out a crude manuscript and found a printer who could pull off the job within my very limited budget.

I was prepared to lose my entire investment in the project and insulate my attic with the thousands of unsold ghost books.

I started taking orders, the printer started printing, and readers started

INTRODUCTION TO SECOND EDITION

GHOST STORIES OF BERKS COUNTY

buying. Before any of us could say "boo," the orders and sales far outraced the printer's capability to keep the books rolling off the presses and into the bindery. Those presses and that binding process, it should be noted, were not too many generations removed from Herr Guttenberg's primitive techniques. And yet, there was a certain charm to it all back then.

There was nothing charming about the many books which came back with pages out of place, missing, or blank.

Nothing was funny about the books which, when opened for the first time, spilled out their pages when the binding glue failed to bind.

And, for the naive and novice writer and self-publisher, there was artistic heartbreak when the final typeset copy bristled with typographical errors. Not all of the misspellings and missed words were my fault. Most, maybe, but not all.

What was worst about the miscues in that first book was what I have called the "lost manuscript pages" in which the first story, "The Ghost on the Throne," comes to a chilling conclusion.

Somehow, at some time, a full three pages were overlooked by the typesetter. The print job was so rushed, under the burden of crude equipment and under the pressure of advance orders and my own impatience, that it was never proofread. I was shocked and angry when I opened the pages of my "baby" for the first time and was peppered by typos and rendered hollow by the missing pages.

I have always likened the publishing of one of my books to giving birth.

It all starts with the idea. From that moment of conception, there are weeks and then months of work, some final days of intense mental and physical labor, and after a nerve-wracking wait, the magical moment the finished product reaches my arms.

I know all along that it will look like most other books, but with its own character and its own personality.

When the first copy arrives from the printer, I hold it, gaze at it interminably, and welcome it into the family.

Back in 1982, upon the "birth" of my first book, there were some birth defects. But, I loved that old ghost book just the same.

INTRODUCTION TO SECOND EDITION

GHOST STORIES OF BERKS COUNTY

Now, a bit farther on in this publishing business, I have the opportunity for some corrective surgery.

The basic text of the book remains the same. Not a word (or a typo) has been changed.

But, you are about to read is the "lost" conclusion of the first story in that first ghost book—the story which ended with (but should not have) these words:

The conversation of just seconds ago was forgotten by both of those who had engaged in it.

Now, in an unearthly, supernatural moment, the culmination of the ghost hunter's search and that widow's dreams had begun.

The eerie magnetism of that place, that night, was like no other experience one could ever imagine.

And now, that experience:

In a vacuum of sound, only the echo of one's heartbeat through the body would break the ungodly quiet.

In an instant, the woman's spell was shattered as she reached to the side of the doorway, turning out the dim ceiling light which had hitherto illuminated the kitchen. At the instant the light went out, Margaret whispered, "My God...My God!"

Her whispers mounted: "My God...My God!!"

"Please...please!"

"Oh, Jacob...JACOB!"

With each intense word, her body was drawn to and through the doorway. While one hand held the screen door open, the other trembled in a limp point toward the rock-seat.

Alone, in a darkening, strange room, the writer's eyes were riveted on the woman and her bizarre soliloquy. For a long instant too terrified to blink, he gathered his senses and turned his attention toward the back yard.

"Oh Jacob....Jacob," the woman continued. Each new pronouncement mellowed and the icy stare toward the yard softened. A smile could be perceived as she continued to call the name into the night.

As the room darkened even more, the moonlight seemed to glow and

INTRODUCTION TO SECOND EDITION

GHOST STORIES OF BERKS COUNTY

reflect off wisps of clouds and across puffs of gray flora on the landscape. As if trying to find excuses for not looking directly at the rock formation, the writer quickly surveyed the setting.

But, a corner of his eye caught a most unexplainable sight.

No form or figure or apparition could be discerned. But, it was as if a shadow was cast by the moonlight, just to the left of the gathering of rocks. There was no identifiable shape to the shadow, and no motion.

The woman's cries were now silenced, and she continued to stare at the rocks. Her smile was that of a satisfied, contented, much younger woman. The moonlight was kind to her face.

Still staring at the strange shadow outside, the writer sensed the woman's face turning toward him. Startled and tingling, he sharply turned and looked at her.

Her smile was withering, and reality seemed to be returning to her bleak expression. Again the writer turned his attention quickly to the rock formation. The rocks, the "throne," and everything around them were aglow with the silvery light of the moon.

The wisps of clouds mounted. They seemed to rush across the sky as if late for an empyreal appointment.

Margaret's words were measured: "Jacob...my beloved Jacob."

With that, the woman swiveled and switched on the kitchen light. Warding off a chill which had been lost in the past moments, she closed the screen door, the inner door, and walked slowly back to the table.

With less conviction and much more unsteadiness, the writer blinked his eyes—perhaps for the first time in many minutes—and addressed himself to the now-cold coffee and cookies.

Waiting for the woman to make the first noteworthy comment after what had been a most incredible experience, the writer peered over his glasses as the woman poured fresh cups of coffee.

"Jacob is such a fine man," she said, and immediately turned her attention to the domestic courtesies at hand.

But the tense of her comment and the tenseness of those few awe-inspiring moments led the writer to believe that the experiences may very well have been the ultimate realization of a ghost hunter's innermost quest.

And I was that writer.

INTRODUCTION TO SECOND EDITION

INTRODUCTION
AND
"THE GHOST OF THE THRONE"

Are the quiet valleys and dark hillsides of the Pennsylvania Dutch Country haunted by the ghosts of Indians, soldiers and less romantic but awe-inspiring spirits?

For centuries, tales of "pow-wowing," "witchcraft" and "voodoo" have been told in the annals of the history and culture of this region, and have sustained themselves through to the lives of the modern descendants of the early pioneer settlers of the area.

Arthur H. Lewis, the celebrated Pennsylvania author-historian, wrote of necromancy in York County and the infamous Blymire "Hex Trial." The Commonwealth's own Bureau of Travel Development spices its travel brochure package with a listing of Pennsylvania "haunted houses," which lists dozens of spirits and tells where to find them. Spine-chilling ghost stories are sure to ignite the imagination of campers, kids and grownups alike as they spend dark nights in the mysteriously magnificent land of the "Pennsylvania Dutch." Even the presence of "hex signs" (although reportedly "chust for nice") adds to the aura of one of America's most superstitious and skeptical regions.

Hard-line "Dutchmen" may quite often visit so-called "powwow" doctors before consulting a physician in even the gravest matters of health. Even today, these faith healers and "witches" practice necromancy in cities, boroughs and rural areas of Berks and other counties. These "doctors" consult such manuals as the powwowers' textbook of sorts, "The Long, Lost Friend," or the "Sixth and Seventh Books of Moses," a volume gleaned from the mosaic books of the Cabala and Talmud.

Beyond powwowers , witches and hex signs, even the present generation "Dutchman" is, to a great extent, superstitious. Thus, ghost stories and legends have been preserved here for decades.

While I shall ultimately take you to a Berks County farmhouse for a close encounter of the ghostly kind — a bizarre account of an actual supernatural experience — let us first examine a sampling of spiritual stories emanating from this enchanted corner of America.

The county is proud of its historical legends. Stories such as the Indian ghost seen by pioneer Christel Neucommer, the suicidal pact of Indians Towkee and Oneeda and their unrestful haunting of "Dragon Cave" do not pass away easily. The county's breadbasket, the Oley Valley, is equally fertile with supernatural stories abounding even to the present day. Historical accounts have touched on ghostly goings-on in the highlands of Hawk Mountain and the Pinnacle, and the once glorious spas of South Mountain near Wernersville continue to generate stories about things that go bump in the night.

Noted ghost hunter and author Hanz Holzer has confirmed the existence of a ghost in one Berks home; Arthur H. Lewis calls "Mountain Mary" Jung, an 18th century herbalist, "Pennsylvania's most famous witch." Berks has its "lovers' leap," a haunted cave, hidden or lost Indian burial grounds, and an incredible array of homes, churches and forests where spooks run freely.

Newspapers in Berks have run accounts of the more fascinating ghost stories. Historians and folklorists have dedicated much time and space to the pursuit of the unknown and unseen.

Shall we now visit one of these places? Shall we imagine the setting — a windswept, moondrenched night on a lonely road near the foot of the fabled South Mountain?

She — let us call her Margaret — was a woman not unlike any you'd expect to find in any average rural farmhouse. Plain, plump and pleasant, she was untying her faded print apron as she answered the door to greet the inquisitive writer.

As the woman typified the corpulent Pennsylvania Dutch widow, so did the home typify the Pennsylvania Dutch dwelling. Simple, functional, with a homely look perfumed by the aroma of freshly-baked goodies. It was over these warm cookies and steaming coffee that we discussed the subject of the visit.

Her husband — let us call him Jacob — departed this life six years before and was buried in a family graveyard a quarter-mile across field and farmyard from the house. Between this final resting place and the home he and Margaret loved so much was a shallow grotto, seeming to be although not carved by human hands. It lay in a cluster of rock just thirty yards from a rear kitchen door and window of the home.

The rockbound chamber provided a natural seat, with an indentation just wide and deep enough for the average fundament. It was on this stony bench where Jacob would idle the time away between home chores and farm work. So popular was it with the old man that Margaret would call it "The Throne." It was not unusual for the man to fall asleep on the "throne," oblivious to the craggly cushion upon which he rested. Only Margaret's call to lunch or dinner would disturb his solace.

It was this "throne" that drew the writer to Margaret's home. Hearing of "strange stories" and unusual occurrences at the farmhouse, the amateur ghost hunter was anxious to meet Margaret and hear her touching story.

Margaret's reception was cordial and completely free of anxiety, suspicion or fear. Fear, however, may have been evident on the face of the writer as the eerie tale of Jacob's ghostly reappearances was calmly and emotionlessly told by the kindly old woman.

If the adage, "people die as they lived" is to be believed, then Jacob would have epitomized this theory. A hard-working individual-

2

ist, Jacob salvaged the farm from years of neglect and through subsequent years of very hard and deliberate work, he would restore it to its century-old charm. The labor of love, as displayed by the childless Jacob and Margaret, manifested itself in the clean, stately home. Through the daylight hours, Jacob would work to farm the fields and perform the routine and emergency chores required around the living quarters. By night, he would talk with Margaret and read his way into a well-deserved sleep.

Jacob walked away from the breakfast table one chilly autumn morning to perform the duties of the harvest in the fields just over a small rise out of sight of the house. For years, it was Jacob's custom to return to the home at least a half-hour past noon for a farmer's lunch. Margaret would employ the alarm of a solid dinnerbell that hung on the back porch to harken a tardy Jacob from the fields. At what she recalls as regular intervals at 12:35, 12:40 and 12:45, Margaret rang the bell calling Jacob to lunch. Another ten minutes went by. Surely Jacob heard the resounding summon as it echoed through the valleys around the farm. And surely the farmer was hungry — Margaret could not recall a single time in their married life when Jacob would be late for any meal sitting.

The time passed, perhaps a half-hour, and Margaret knew what she had to do. An ethereal knowledge gripped the woman and drew her to her fateful task. Although there was no way for her to know the scene she was about to find, a supernatural feeling wrapped aound her thoughts and prepared her for the most dreaded moment a devoted wife would ever experience.

Margaret slipped on a sweater and headed toward the rise just past the familiar "throne." Reaching the crest of the hillock, she looked across the field below and saw her beloved Jacob slumped over a piece of farm machinery, breathless and motionless. As if prepared for the grim finding, Margaret breathed a mournful sigh and slowly approached the melancholy scene. Kneeling by her fallen mate, Margaret clutched his head and shoulder, gave a whimper of grief and placed a farewell kiss on Jacob's cold temple.

"Jacob was not dead," says the woman today, "he had merely gone into a new and distant place." Not particularly religious, but a self-proclaimed "God-fearing Christian," Margaret said she and Jacob were not permanently separated, merely temporarily estranged by the earthly departure.

From the time Margaret discovered her deceased husband, to the present day, she was sure Jacob would be able to maintain contact with her. He would return to the quiet farmhouse on the call of the pealing bell. He would return to his throne and assure Margaret that he awaited her entry into the world he had entered, but could not describe.

It was to witness one of these visitations that the writer went to Margaret's home. There had been reports of more than one reputable neighbor or curious spy hearing the plaintive echo of the dinner bell.

And, if Margaret was to be believed, Jacob would return and stare toward the house from the rocky throne.

Margaret was assured the ghostly return would not be treated as a "side show." Complete respect and sincerity would be maintained, and both location and identification would remain untold.

Margaret could not explain why the image of her husband returned not at the noon hour during which he passed away but durng nights of the full moon; nor could she recall exactly how and when the hauntings began. Calmly, she accepted the spectral presence. Calmly but cautiously, she would discuss the matter with the eager writer.

But this evening was to consist of more than simple discussion. A full moon shone overhead, and for the first time, Margaret was to share her apparitional mate with an outsider.

There was no guarantee when, or if, Jacob would visit that particular night. Margaret could recall vaguely that the visits would take place almost invariably before midnight. The visit would be short, but ever so meaningful. It would merely be the entrance of the spectre, a brief roost on the "throne" and a ghostly passing of the dead man's figure into the night. Jacob would return in the farm clothes he wore when Margaret found him lifeless in yonder field. He would utter no sounds, show no expression, make no motion. His ghost would slip silently into and out of the darkness with little fanfare.

From the corner of the writer's eye, through the back door screen, the "throne" was visible — its rocky white figure breaking the dull milky-black night. It was obvious that Margaret kept herself positioned so that she could readily view the stage upon which the wraith would play.

Margaret was not eager to discuss the ghostly effects that were to take place — those effects of which the writer was so interested. No, Margaret would sway the conversation to that of God, heaven, the Commandments and the rewards of life lived by the Golden Rule. She would seem to seek a closeness to God that night, as if trying to establish an intimacy with her departed husband. She would mold earthly and heavenly life as one. Her verbal scenario would allow little delineation between celestial and earthbound happiness. She would establish an aura that would grip the room and this writer in a suspenseful, emotional, almost electrical mood.

As the woman and the writer bandied about various topics over cooling coffee and half-eaten cookies, the conversation slowed and lapsed as a strange sensation permeated the kitchen air. A blind gaze locked the woman's eyes toward the doorway and pulled her toward the slightly-ajar kitchen door. Margaret's skin was bleached and her face distressed. As if every sense was numbed, she mechanically positioned herself at the doorway, eyes affixed toward the yard and the formation of rocks. The conversation of just seconds ago was forgotten by both of those who had engaged in it. Now, in an unearthly, supernatural moment, the culmination of the ghost hunter's search and the widow's dreams had begun. The eerie magnetism of that place, that night, was like no other experience one could ever imagine.

THE GHOSTS OF THE "ECK"

Research and Personal Interviews
February, 1982

From its first human settlers to those who choose to call it home today, what we now call Hawk Mountain has been one of the most enigmatic regions of Berks County. It is a place where what is natural and what is supernatural occupy the same space. It is where fact and fantasy intertwine and emerge as legend.

Hawk Mountain, which stretches from Bailey's Crossing and Eckville to its lofty peak near the county line, has seemed to nurture these legends through the stories told by its people. And, it may be that many of these "legends" are products of mere happenstance, supposition, or superstition. Maurice Broun, who we shall meet in more depth later in this chapter, called the tales told by those mountain folk "Middle Age superstitions." But let us register in our mental notebook that the illustrious Mr. Broun was a proper Bostonian transplanted to the mountain, and was pragmatically unwilling to immerse himself in the Pennsylvania "Dutch" way of the occult. Powwowing, hexing and witchcraft has played a role in life in this part of the county since before the white man's incursion, and in its way, continues today.

Setting the stage for the baffling ghost stories of Hawk Mountain, we shall look back at some of the less monumental yet equally baffling stories which have been etched in the annals of the "eck."

The stories come from some of the older residents of the "eck," or corner, of the county. Once their trust is gained, their tales are discharged from memories tainted, perhaps, by time, but vivid in detail and sincerity.

They called Matthias Berger (or Berg, or Bergh) "the monk." They say he came up from Reading to the mountain to get away from the pressures of city life. For nearly three decades, the monk lived an ascetic existence in a crude shack on the slope of the mountain. They say he brewed mountain tea from goldenrod. Mountain folks were inclined to believe he was a holy man of sorts, and they'd bring their children to his hermitage to be baptised. Some folks say he erected a large oak cross in a clearing near his shack, upon which he'd drape his body and scream into the forest in a foreign tongue, believed to be Latin. This pious, gentle man met a most unfortunate fate on the mountain. They say "the monk" was murdered by an unknown person, and his body, or what was left of it, was found on Owl's Head, the bones picked clean by turkey vultures!

Another mysterious man of the mountain was Manassas Camp. Manassas lived in a log cabin near the Pine Swamp at the foot of the mountain and tended a charcoal burner deep in the woods. Manassas Camp's story adds spice to the mountain's mystical menu, and provides an apparational appetizer for the main course yet to be served.

One day, six blasts of a shotgun were heard echoing through the foothills. The shots were traced to Manassas Camp, who told of seven devils that came to him from the Pine Swamp. He shot six of them, but the seventh tormented him, saying it would let him live in peace only after one of his children had died. A few days later, a local doctor paid a cabin call on the Camp camp, and found a child's body suspended above a table by a muslin cloth, so the rats wouldn't get at it.

A man from Eckville relates this next bizarre story. The gent was returning home after dark, and as he approached his house he saw the figure of a woman walking through his front door. And we mean THROUGH his front door! He thought it was his wife in a somnambulatory stroll. He rushed inside the home and saw his spouse snug and safe in bed. The next day, he tried his best to relate the strange story to what he figured would be skeptical neighbors. The neighbors absorbed his story, turned to each other in disbelief, and told the man that they, too, had seen the same figure at his house on other occasions, but were reluctant to tell anyone!

The road which leads from the valley below to the top of Hawk Mountain has harbored its own harrowing yarns since it evolved from a deer path to an Indian trail to a two-lane macadam road. In recent years, passers-by have reported numerous strange events. Near the Hawk Mountain Sanctuary complex atop the mountain, a man told others of driving by the sanctuary headquarters and having his car forced off the road by a bright light. He was so frightened that he even told State Police troopers he saw what appeared to be the ghost of a ten-foot tall man! A similar story from a less lofty locale will follow.

As information for this book was being gathered, the next unexplainable event took place near the sanctuary complex. A family was passing the buildings en route to a day with nature. Sanctuary officials

6

were told that as the family car passed the former headquarters building, the four-year old girl inside shuddered, telling her mommy she
was scared. Pointing to the simple white building, she said, "Mommy,
there's a ghost in that house!"

Out of the mouth of babes . . . . .

The mind is teased with the following account. Only the reader
can reckon — is it coincidence or the manipulation of an unseen,
unearthly force? In 1975, the present curator of the sanctuary relates,
five men each living within a couple miles of each other all on the same
side of the roading leading to the sanctuary within a two-month period
each lost a parent who died unexpectedly!

While not related to the supernatural, some other stories about the
mountain warrant inclusion in this overview of a most intriguing place.
For example, during prohibition, the former sanctuary headquarters
was rented to a group of "bootleggers" who allegedly made bathtub
gin in the basement. In 1930, the illegal still on the hill was raided by
"revenooers" who found their prey difficult to snatch. A brief gun battle
raged at the old mountain house before the bootleggers were taken
into custody.

The colorful history of Hawk Mountain continues into the 1940s,
when it was reported that State Police and F.B.I. agents had their eyes
on the mountain as a suspected Nazi sympathizers' stronghold!
Birders with binoculars reflecting from the lookouts were enemy spies
signalling comrades at mythical ammunition dumps deep in the forest.
Tourists and nature lovers with exotic auto license plates ascending to
the burgeoning sanctuary were out-of-towners up to no good!

As outrageous as some of the lore of Hawk Mountain may be,
there is one story which has been perpetuated in the memories of the
handful of mountain men and women still alive and willing to tell it, and
in the precious few books detailing life on the mountain.

It is the story of Matthias Schambacher.

The Schambachers, Margaret and Matthias, moved to the mountain in the middle of the 19th century. Matthias transformed the old
Jacob Gerhardt stone home into a kind of wayside tavern, making and
selling applejack and Blue Mountain tea to travelers using the road
over the mountain as an avenue of commerce from the coal regions to
the Lehigh Valley. Most of these included peddlers and deliverymen,
who would be anxious to stop at Schambacher's for refreshment. But,
as the stories go, some never made it any further.

Schambacher is not painted as a pleasant man. Local children
were warned to steer clear of him. If they encountered him, they'd run
in utter fear. Whatever kind of husband and father he may have been,
he developed a terrible reputation which was only to further degener-
ate as he grew older.

According to published accounts, Schambacher's tavern was from its beginning held in suspicion. Horses shied away from, and in some cases bolted from the barn which stood across the road from the tavern. It was in this barn that a passerby hearing low moaning eminating from the barn, opened a door and found Schambacher with hatchet in hand. The tavernkeeper threatened the man, who ran in fear to tell his story to friends in the valley. And, it was in this barn that splotches of fresh blood were found by another tavern patron.

Quite simply, Matthias Schambacher was suspected of murdering about eleven men. We say "about" because nobody is really sure how many were lured into a drinking spree at the tavern and butchered in the barn, or indeed if any ever were. It is recorded that Schambacher was seen wearing and selling used Civil War uniforms a few weeks after a used Civil War uniform peddler was reported missing somewhere between Orwigsburg and Kempton. And, Schambacher was a genuine suspect in the murder of Albany Township herb doctor George Saylor. Local citizens were so convinced that the tavernkeeper was guilty that they threatened to blow up the mountaintop house. Their self-styled "necktie party" was halted by the efforts of a local constable.

In his last few months of life on earth, Matthias Schambacher's state of mind deterioriated to the point that he allegedly "spilled his guts" to certain visitors, confessing his guilt.

Probably the most likely spirit to haunt the "eck" would be that of Matthias Schambacher. Wild tales have continued to circulate, and have vaulted the allegations about this tavernkeeper into legend. From the day of his death to the present, all things of substance left to perpetuate the man's reputation seem to have their own stories attached to them. We've recounted the suspected happenings within the old tavern itself. And it is said that the night of Schambacher's burial, bolts of lightning repeatedly struck the fresh grave. Local folks still report odd occurrences at Schambacher's grave — some seeing a strange glow hovering over the simple tombstone, others speaking of mysterious visitors who linger at the gravesite and stare down at old Schambacher and disappear over the ridge of the New Bethel Church graveyard.

From that graveyard, which extends along a broad hillside next to what one writer has called one of the most impressive churches in the world, we suspect another ghostly tale drew its first breath.

Travelling through the picturesque hills of Albany Township, several people told the inquiring ghost hunter that they've heard bits and pieces of the Schambacher story. One man, however, provides one story which defies explanation.

The old-timer from Kempton claims that even today, screaming and moaning can be heard wafting down from the mountains of the "eck." When reminded of the great birds that call the mountan home, or use it as a way-station, the man is quick to assure us that the sounds are "not of this world."

8

While many, if not most ghost stories seem to be set at night, this one took place under blue sky and a chilly late-winter sun.

The man was driving his tractor slowly along the road which leads to the New Bethel Church when he was temporarily blinded by a sudden flash of light. It seemed to illuminate the whole countryside, he says, but centered itself along the road. He slammed on the brakes and pulled to the side of the road ever so slowly. As he regained his senses and his vision, he was taken by a strange glow moving down the road toward him. It was about ten feet tall and moved very slowly. At first, he thought it was a fog, mist or some other earthly or meteorological phenomenon, but that thought was quickly dashed.

The old man saw the glow gradually develop into what he swore was the shape of a man. For a brief moment, he saw arms and legs take definite form. Perhaps two seconds after they formed, the glow ceased. It simply vanished, as they say, into thin air!

The man had not been drinking, nor was he excessively tired. Nor had he ever had any particular belief in, or experience with, ghosts. After this unexplained vision, however, he became quite committed to the possibility. And still today, his voice quivers as he repeats his story.

There is a similar story told by another old Albany Township man who will also relate his experience only if coaxed. He's another man with furrowed forehead and leathery hands toughened by years of farm work. Another proud man with no reason to make up a "ghost story."

Again let us note that the day was sunny, but a late winter's chill was in the air. This scenario will be a factor which may tie each of these stories together. Again the man was slowly making his way along the road leading past the New Bethel Church. But this time, no spectacular flash of light — no eerie glow. Simply an old man, nattily yet simply dressed, walking along the shoulder of the road. His shoulders were slumped, head cast downward in a kind of melancholy tramping. Believing he may have known the man, the driver took particular notice of the walker. But for a moment, only a fraction of a second perhaps, his attention was diverted from the man who had been ambling alongside the road. When he turned back to have a closer look at the man, no one was there. The spectre had disappeared. The man was dumbfounded, and quickly surveyed the area, trying to find a place where the hiker may have escaped to. But there was no high corn in the field, no nearby woods, no ditches or buildings. Nothing in, behind, or under which a man could hide. Perplexed, the man glanced in his rear-view mirror and nearly drove off the road! There, walking far behind him, was the same figure he had seen not two seconds before an equal distance in front of him. The figure was walking away from him, and he managed to keep it in his sight until once again he felt the pulsation of fear envelop his body. As he watched the figure grow smaller in perspective, it faded from view, as if to simply vanish, shall we say again, into thin air!

And, oh yes, did I tell you WHEN each of these experiences took place? Did I tell you when the two old men, who by the way were familiar with each other's names but were not acquaintances, saw the apparitions? Well, they both told me "sometime in early March." And did I tell you when Matthias Schambacher died? March 10th, 1879!

We will never know if the experiences of the two men are linked to Schambacher, or if the glow or phanton hiker was indeed Matthias Schambacher's spirit. But we do know that Schambacher's infamy is likely to play a role in the legend of Berks County's "eck" forever.

A self-proclaimed "medium" who visited the mountain near the one-hundredth anniversary of Schambacher's death substantiated that statement somewhat, and yet gave evidence that any such spirit haunting the old mountaintop tavern may not be that of the alleged evil-doer, but one of another person who could be considered the social opposite of Schambacher. She acknowledges that Schambacher's "presence" is felt all around the mountain and throughout the "eck," but says his spirit is trapped within his grave. It is not the ghost of Matthias Schambacher which haunts the former tavern, and hot that of any of the men allegedly slain by its former proprietor. No, the spirit inside the home is that of a very young girl who supposedly met an untimely, agonizing and unexplained death in the building sometime in the late eighteenth century. The identity of the girl, and any documentation that she indeed ever existed, remains unclear. And details of her life and her death are likely to remain unattainable, perhaps even through psychic or spiritual means. According to the researcher, the young girl was a deaf-mute, and her spirit remains in a kind of limbo.

There are indications that the girl died a slow death, perhaps of starvation, after her parents died. According to the woman who sensed the spirit of the hapless waif, she was left to fend for herself inside the house, and without her parents to help her, perished. Her spirit remmains earthbound, never able to pass into the "other side." This is the spirit now inhabiting the Schambacher house. It is a spirit which took up residence there, so to speak, perhaps seventy-five years before Schambacher's alleged murders. Could it be the spirit of the house even then led Schambacher to evil? Could his mind have been affected by the innocent, yet frightening haunting of a pathetic four year old deaf-mute girl? They are questions to ponder.

Whatever, the medium said she "couldn't get past the strong spirit of the young girl" and into the matter of Matthias Schambacher. In fact, she suggested that no one ever attempt to exorcise the child's spirit from the house lest the unpredictable spirit of Schambacher be allowed to infest the place.

On the occasion of the medium's visit to the mountain, several college students interested in the supernatural listened to the researcher's revelations. One student who had read about Schambacher's alleged crimes noted that he was suspected of burying some of his victims near a persimmon tree which was still standing near the home. Another student asked if they could walk outside to this site.

The medium accommodated the students and, joined by the present occupant of the house, started outside across the yard. Suddenly, in mid-stride, the researcher screamed to stop! The group watched as she started to shake, and told them it was far too dangerous to go any closer to the persimmon tree. She was overcome by what she described as an "evil feeling," and refused to continue walking, or elaborate on the source or substance of the feeling.

The medium's sensitivity on Hawk Mountain was not limited to the spirit of the little girl and the presence of Schambacher. Early on, she detected the feeling that the Indians had held the mountain in high esteem. She said she could sense tribal leaders holding council meetings near the house. She felt the sanctity of the mountain and the respect given to it by the natives. She could sense a "circle" of Indian chiefs carrying out a ceremony of some kind, in an area near a pond next to the house.

The eyebrows of at least one person in attendance then raised in incredulity. The present curator of the sanctuary, recalling excavating work done in the 1960's when an orchard next to Schambacher's was converted into the pond, remembered the discovery of the archeological remains of an Indian ceremonial ring. Evidence of rock configurations and fire led to the belief that they had uncovered this place where the most sacred of Indian rituals were carried out. And, according to the curator, the finding was kept low key. There were no written records of it, only the memories of those who were there. The medium, therefore, had virtually no way of knowing about it.

It would seem appropriate that the mountain would be special to the natives of the mountain. And yes, it is widely held that the peaks of what we call the Pinnacle and Hawk Mountain were said to be sacred to the Lenni Lenape Indians who called them home. It was the white man's intrusion onto this land which led to the massacre of a family which in turn led to the building of what became Schambacher's home and tavern.

In the mid-eighteenth century, the Indians were more or less at peace with the white settlers who ventured onto the foothills of the Blue Mountains. But relations deteriorated as promises and treaties were broken and the Indians were shoved deeper into the forests, away from the fertile soil of the valleys. The natives responded by attacking forts and settlements along the mountain ridge.

The earliest tragedy to take place on or near Hawk Mountain occurred in 1756. In February of that year, all but one member of the Gerhardt family were slaughtered by Indians. The only survivor, Jacob, watched from nearby underbrush as the Indians called his father from the cabin, killed him and set fire to the home. The eleven-year old boy lost his parents and five brothers and sisters in the ensuing catastrophe.

Jacob went on to build the "cottage" on the mountain in 1793, and for nearly sixty years, the property remained in the Gerhardt family name. On a parcel of that land, George and Priscilla Bolich rebuilt a structure on the slope of the 1,500-foot mountain. The Bolichs resided at the lonely site for 52 years, eventually selling out to Margaret and Matthias Schambacher.

Strange sounds inside the old Schambacher homestead have been reported since the beginning of the twentieth century. In fact, from almost the first day of the building's inclusion in the Hawk Mountain Sanctuary fold, naturalists have tried to explain the mysterious clamorings as just the sounds of nature — and not the supernatural.

The September 25, 1938 Reading EAGLE detailed the announcement of the acquisition of the Schambacher home by Mrs. Raymond V. Ingersoll of Brooklyn, New York. Mrs. Ingersoll presented the building as a gift to the Hawk Mountain Sanctuary Association, which had just purchased 1,400 acres of mountain land from a lumber company through the fund-raising efforts of Mrs. C. N. Edge, also of New York City.

The establishment of the sanctuary came as good news to the conservationists of the area. And, one of the first organizations to recognize the foresight of those who gave time and money to make the sanctuary a reality was the Baird Ornithological Society of Reading. Its president in 1938 was Reading Museum assistant curator Earle Poole, who told a delighted membership that the Schambacher building would be renovated for use as "a rendezvous for bird lovers." As reported in the EAGLE article entitled, "Mystery of Haunted Hawk Mountain House Is Solved," Mr. Poole attempted to do just that and assuage an audience undoubtedly apprehensive about the reported goings-on at the house.

Poole acknowledged that hikers and mountain folk had long avoided the former home of the alleged murderer. He admitted there had been reports of sounds of undetermined origin inside the place. But he had answers. Poole said a search of the property revealed no well, which was supposed to have been the dumping site of the body of one of Schambacher's victims. He added that the "strange sounds" of Schambacher's were not those of wraiths, but of rats! Wood rats, he said, which had found their way into the basement and walls of the old place.

In his fine book, "Hawks Aloft," Maurice Broun, the renowned environmentalist and naturalist, dedicated an entire chapter to "The Ghosts of Schaumboch's." (We should note that the use of "Schaumboch's" vice "Schambacher's" is prevalent in most written information issued by the Sanctuary, with Broun saying the former version is the one most popular among the mountain folk. "Schambacher," is, as Broun does indicate, the correct spelling of the name.)

In any event, Broun's chapter on the ghosts turns out to have been written with tongue firmly planted in cheek, and quickly disspells all spectral notions with the "wood rat" theme. Maurice and Irma Broun took up residence in the run-down building in the summer of 1938 and almost immediately were beset with things going bump in the night. Suspecting a rational source, Broun commenced to search in ceilings

12

and floorboads for the perpetrators of these nocturnal knocks. In short order, a nest was discovered. Then, a cave rat. And more. And any such supernatural origin of the noises was discounted by the practical Mr. Broun.

The present curator of the sanctuary quips that he doesn't blame Broun for coming up with such an explanation. "Living up there all alone, with no phone, electricity, nothing," he says, "I'd try to be practical about an explanation about mysterious noises, too!"

But more recent inhabitants of the old tavern are not as quick to attribute the sounds they've heard to rodents. The simple bumps and scratching noises by day and night have been accompanied by more vocal manifestations. And, there is some evidence that the well which supposedly serves as a tomb for one of the mountain murder victims does, in fact, exist.

The present curator of the sanctuary, himself a resident of the Schambacher place for many years, says the property was in the hands of the William Turner family around the turn of the century. And, it is said that one of the Turner children actually uncovered the deep watery grave pit, now dry and hidden under thick underbrush and a rotting slate well cover. What's more, human remains — a skull and some bones — were found inside the well! Truth or tale? No one knows for sure, but the curator today swears the location of the well and its grisly contents is a secret known only to him, and he'll never reveal the whereabouts.

The man who currently lives in the Schambacher home inherited the keys to the place as part of the arrangement which brought him to work at the sanctuary. Living there rent-free, he has made the building a rustic, comfortable home. While the glories of nature bristle all around the property, the more domestic sounds of this young man in his solitary — yet anything but lonely — existence fill the inside of Schambacher's. Appointed with tasteful artwork, warmed by a crackling fire and littered only by scholarly books and unfurnished nature notebooks, the home is inviting and intriguing. Not knowing the legend of Matthias Schambacher and what may or may not have happened on the property, one would hail the home as a quiet hideaway far above the murmur and turmoil of civilization. But knowing the Schambacher stories and the importance the Indians placed upon the area, one can then sense a feeling of history as they enter the property. It could be described as a tingling feeling of anticipation — that perhaps a long-unanswered question is about to be resolved. The feeling wraps around physical self, and dissolves deeply into the heart and soul of anyone who spends a few hours atop the mountain.

While anyone with a fertile imagination and a sense of endearment to this lofty island of mystery in a sea of reality may sense these titillating emotions on Hawk Mountain, perhaps only those who reside on the mountain can appreciate, confirm and relate those same emotions.

Since the establishment of the sanctuary, those who have been caretakers of the Schambacher house have been literate men. Those who have passed have recorded their experiences in published journals and books. Still today, the man who walks the same floors and dines on the same table-top as Matthias Schambacher more than a century ago, records his days' events in a journal. "Nature notes," he calls them. And while these annotations document the events of the mountain's natural world, what you are about to read is a chronicle of the unexplained — the mountain's supernatural world.

It is a world which has puzzled generations of men, women and children who have lived on the summits, glens and foothills of the mountain. A veil of mystery cradles this section of the county. Its people harbor their tales of what has, or may have happened there. It is a world apart from the general makeup of the rest of the land which connects it politically with Berks County. It was one of America's first frontiers, with documented battles between the native Americans and those who settled here. In addition to the Gerhardt family story told earlier in this chapter, there are further tales of massacres, bloody murders perpetrated by both red and white men. There are stories of Gypsy encampments in the shadow of the mountain. Stories of pioneer forts, Indian burial grounds. Cave-dwellers and hermits. Bodies found and never claimed or identified. Suicides. Mystery.

In his 1924 book, "More Allegheny Episodes," folklorist Henry W. Shoemaker paints a glorious picture of the Bethel Church, the final resting place of Matthias Schambacher. Shoemaker likens the setting to the French Alps, while frankly discussing its stark simplicity: "How straight and severe and high it stands. How devoid of frills, or frescoes, or other outward ornamentation! How typical of the pioneer life, with its privations, struggles and disappointments. How filled with the gloom of unfulfilled ambitions and dreams."

Shoemaker makes no mention of Schambacher or the legend which developed around him. But, he alludes to the riddles of the "eck." He writes, "Many are the old-time legends which cling to Bethel Church, tales of Indian warfare, panthers, wolves, wild pigeons, Civil War days, ghosts, goblins, love and sorrow, witches and robbers, the whole gamut of mountain life. On the 'green' beyond the churchyard that slopes down toward Pine Creek, the Indians tarried in early days . . the Gypsies have camped there since the Indians abandoned it."

Strange stories revolving around the gypsies weave through the folklore of the mountains, and even today bands of the now-motorized nomads still pass through the deep valleys in and around the "eck."

Let us not confuse the matter, however. Lifting the grim pall we've just cast over the mountain, let us add that this same "eck" is home to many good people. These hard-working folks, many or most of German stock, live and work on the slopes of Hawk Mountain. They farm the land there, and worship and play in this, their chosen home. And this is the norm. The bizarre accounts over the years are very, very thin slices of life there. Similar stories are spread throughout any area. But so many extraordinary events and legends in one compact and quite ordinary locale we call the "eck" require a more than cursory glimpse into them.

Sitting inside the Schambacher home, it is easy to capture the isolation annd remoteness of the mountain 150 years ago. But for the speed of modern automobiles and relative smoothness of macadam roadways, the mountain is still a remote land. The presence of the sanctuary and the lure of its hawks and other attractions have given the mountain a daytime vitality. But the nocturnal atmosphere on the mountain is not unlike what it was a century and a half ago. The night's silence is broken only by the occasional whirr of a car which passes facelessly, and by the unpredictable sound of the wilds.

Having studied the bounty of nature, and having lived within this natural environment for several years, the current resident of Schambacher's is more familiar than most of us with the sounds of nature. Even the most peculiar and unnerving sounds of the forest can be quickly and accurately discerned by this man who has made the natural world his chosen life's work and life style. But again, even he was not prepared for the contributions made by the SUPERnatural forces which play a role in life on Hawk Mountain.

The end of a work day for our subject generally brought a peaceful time during which the events of the day would be recounted and recorded. And, our next story begins during this tranquil time.

"I was typing my nature notes in one corner of the kitchen," he tells us, "and I could feel this presence, over my shoulder . . . it was an eerie feeling. It wasn't there all the time, but it happened now and then." This inexplicable "presence" distracted the young man from his writing, as he tried to reason with himself as to what had brought on the feeling. But accompaying this feeling was something which would strike fear into his being. The intense quiet of the mountain was broken only by the rhythmic typing. But as he went on, circumventing the initial eerie feelings around him, the typing was joined by another sound. From somehwere, he heard a scream! A high-pitched scream. He turned to see who or what may have caused it, but found nothing. It came from the older part of the Schambacher house, but the exact origin could not be pinpointed.

More and more through the next months, similar sounds would be heard. Again, let us remember that this man is trained in the ways of the natural world. He knows the calls of birds. He knows the sounds of the beasts and creatures that inhabit the rocks and rills around him. But neither he nor few others are prepared or equipped to explain the frightening sounds which were to become more and more commonplace. These sounds would not particularly be eminating from outside the house. They could not be placed in any one corner, in any wall or ceiling beam. They were not of this world. Often, the muted sounds of screams were followed by two-way conversation muffled as if coming from another room. And, while the conversation could be heard quite clearly, the words were not understandable.

"The screams are in the house, but they're in the background," relates the man who has heard them all too often. "It's not like if I would scream right now and you would hear it. It does not resonate throughout the rooms. It's off in the back, almost like a cat's meow in the distance. And then it seems to be followed by the conversation. But you can never understand the words. And it always seems to take a second for me to realize what is happening. It's sounds, not really words, much more audible than the screams. And it's much more in the present, or close to you. They're right there — and when you go to listen harder, they're gone!"

Each time, of course, the screams and muffled conversation would strike a note of confusion, if not fear. And yet, knowng the history of the Schambacher place and the legends of the mountain, our subject found a way to cope with the clamorous experience.

Another pesty problem faced by the home's current resident is one reported by others who have lived at Schambacher's. And, while seeming to be somewhat mundane, even this takes on a new wrinkle. The problem is that of flickering electrical lights inside the house. Such a problem is not uncommon to many homes, and has been explained and remedied. But an incident experienced by the man living there now may be more unexplainable than anything that has passed.

"The first time it happened to me I was in the kitchen doing the dishes and it frightened the hell out of me," the story goes. "For some reason I was thinking of coming into the living room and reading, and I was getting done with the dishes. And just when I had finished, I turned around and I was wiping my hands. I happened to look over by the refrigerator where the light switch is, and there it went — off! It went off right in front of my face! I saw the switch go. The switch itself went down. Well, I just stood there frozen for a minute. It was the only light lit that night, so I was in pitch darkness. After I gathered myself, I walked over and flicked the light switch back on, and went into the living room."

It should be pointed out that the light switch is one of the traditional "click" type, which requires some kind of force to turn on and off, as opposed to the newer "mercury" switches which glide up and down with relative ease.

But by far the most terrifying experience the current housetender has had took place, believe it or not, on the night of the 100th anniversary of Matthias Schambacher's death. We shall relate the story as told to us, and you can be the judge as to its fact, fiction or fantasy.

The young man was in the living room of the house, with the two young sons of the sanctuary's curator, who was out of town on business. The three were playing a board game on the floor of a dimly-lit parlor.

"All of a sudden, we heard what sounded like someone walking across the back porch — five or six steps. It seems that they got right behind the back door (which leads from the living room to the porch) and you could hear shuffling noises, or a little skirmish, or somebody trying to get away from somebody else." At this point, he admits that his imagination may have begun to run wild, but swears, "we heard a sharpening sound and a whoosh through the air and something — a thud — hitting the deck, rolling a bit, and falling off the porch!"

All of this happened within a minute or so. "It was as if time was suspended," he recalls. Whatever, the terrified trio scurried to the front door and ran across the street and up the hill to the curator's home.

And so, the legends of Hawk Mountain and the "eck" continue to grow and thrive. The medium who visited the mountain in 1979 was given few, if any clues to any of the lore of the land. And yet, she built a story around the "presence" of a malevolent sprit (Schambacher?) and a young girl. Some feel the younger spirit may be that of one of the Jacob Gerhardt family, which lived in the home durng the period described in the medium's contact with the spirit. Nonetheless, the spirits contacted by the woman led to the bolstering of one legend and the creation of another. And, for all who hold the mountain in awe, her observations added more fuel to the fires of their imaginations. And, the repercussions of her visit continue to rattle the nerves of many of those who were present during her visit. Her "visions" have at once expanded, enriched and perhaps exaggerated the lore of Hawk Mountain.

"This whole 'eck' of the county is a magical, mysterious, weird area of Berks." With those words, the curator of the Hawk Mountain Sanctuary offers his gut feelings about this land which has captured the imaginations of generations of Berks Countains.

But even more than capturing imaginations, this "eck," this corner of the county has maintained a special kind of grip on those who care enough and try hard enough to understand it. Those who visit here can only stand on the outside looking into this bewitched land. But those who have lived there are the only ones who can truly appreciate the aura which girdles the area. There is no silence at this quiet place. Even in the middle of a cold, winter night, the breeze sweeps through the trees — ever so gently, perhaps, but the mountain seems to be eternally awash with the wind. Civilization is all around the valleys below, pinpoints of light on distant planes. But below, immediately below, a strange, luminous mist dots the dark panorama. The mist and sudden, unexplainable sounds of the night can probably be explained as simple atmospheric conditions. But the feeling one feels and the sensations one senses are never to be explained.

Again we turn to the curator of the sanctuary, who takes a cautious approach to those sensations and feelings: "I've been on that mountain since 1948. You can just feel it. Something strong is overwhelming you. My grandfather was a powwow doctor and once he took us kids to a furnace where he worked. He said he'd show us the devil inside the furnace. He opened the door and damned if we didn't see a figure . . .

crouched down . . . laughing at us! My grandfather slammed the door.

"Up here, I've seen that same thing. I've seen it walking up the road at night. I've looked over and have seen it. Maybe it's must my imagination, but . . . . ."

His words trailed off, but his thoughts regrouped as his supernatural experiences on the mountain flashed before him. "I don't want to believe too strongly in this stuff," he adds, "because I never want to leave this wonderful mountain!"

A MANIFESTATION NEAR MOHRSVILLE

— Published Newspaper Accounts
February 1982

Young Adaline Baver was the "belle" of central Berks County. She lived on a farm somewhere near the sleepy town of Mohrsville, close to the Schuylkill Canal, the Reading Railroad tracks and the Pottsville-to-Reading turnpike. Later in her life, and after her life, these three arteries would play major roles in one of the county's most mysterious and astonishing ghost stories.

On the night of October 14, 1845, Catherine Seaman of Leesport was on her job at the Mohrsville Hotel. The lodge was quite busy that particular evening because the Berks County Fair was underway in Reading. Travellers from miles around would park their buggies at the Mohrsville Inn and continue to the big city by rail.

That night, Catherine was performing her duties in the hotel's tavern, and found that the supply of a certain foodstuff had been depleted. A new supply was available downstairs, in the cellar of the hotel. So, Catherine Seaman walked outside through a side door and into the basement.

From the gloomy canal towpath nearby, Catherine could hear the faint, ghastly moaning of what she believed was a young girl. She returned inside the hotel and in horror, told the proprietor of the unearthly utterings. He consoled her, saying it was probably the inebriated wailing of the "salty dogs" aboard a canal boat. Catherine's fear, and the entire matter, went overlooked through the remainder of the night.

As the sun signalled another day, a deaf-mute tramp, happily wandering along the rails of the Reading near the hotel, was shocked by the discovery of the body of a young girl — face down in the muddy bank of the canal. He ran to the nearby hotel and tried to explain his finding to the hosteler and Catherine Seaman. His frantic, silent motions were in vain however, since neither could understand the vagabond's sign language.

A few hours later a repair gang from the railroad made the grisly discovery. They came to the hotel, explained their finding and summoned help. The workers, the innkeeper, Catherine Seaman and the

18

voiceless tramp went to the scene and the body was identified.

The murdered girl was Adaline Baver. Her throat had been slashed. And it became clear to the hotel's proprietor and Catherine Seaman that the terrible moanings the previous evening were apparently from the girl, as an unidentified murderer ended her short life. The killer vanished into the countryside and was never brought to justice. A Samuel Heilner of Minersville, seen with Miss Baver the day of the murder, was charged with the crime, but was found innocent.

We turn now to a contemporary newspaper account of the Adaline Baver murder for added depth:

The place of death was said to have been on Heffner's Island, in the confines of Centre Township . . . Having been over the ground, our theory of the murder is this, and we think, future discovery, should it be made, will show that we are not far from wrong.

Someone possessing her confidences, who had made an engagement, possibly, to meet her at Mohrsville, or who had induced her to come there to find a home as help in some family, was, we think, concerned in the murder.

The person(s) guilty of this most atrocious deed was not a stranger to the locality, as the body was found in a deep hole, where, had it sunk permanently, would perhaps not been found for weeks. This hole was doubtless known to the murderer much deeper than any water in the Schuylkill in that vicinity. If but one person was concerned in this business, a truck was used for the body's conveyance down the rail road to the Irish Creek Bridge, as no one man could be supposed to carry a body weighing 150 or more pounds 3/4 mile from the murder scene. We think the girl was killed about noon, her body left in the hollow described until late in the night, when it was conveyed on a truck to the place it was found.

She, whose funeral was the saddest known in the vicinity, had much beside the manner of her death to cause touching reminiscences on the part of the large attendance at her funeral. She was a beautiful girl, of amiable disposition, which sought never to offend, whose life was, under those circumstances, and in life's morning, by the hand of a murderer taken away.

And so, the Berks and Schuylkill JOURNAL newspaper offers its graphic and daring account of the murder of Adaline Baver.

Act two:
Three decades later.
Near Mohrsville.

The scene is set along the turnpike from Pottsville to Reading — now the "old road" from Shoemakersville to Mohrsville. The characters: James Daubley, Henry Schmeck . . . and Adaline Baver!

At about 10 p.m., somewhere between Shoemakersville and Mohrsville on a balmy early June evening, Daubley and Schmeck were in a carriage on the turnpike. Daubley, a horse buyer from Montgomery County, was in the Central Berks area on a buying mission. Schmeck, a hired man, was behind the reins.

As the buggy passed through the woodland between the two villages, Daubley reported in a Reading newspaper on June 7, "My horse gave a start as a bright object skipped across the road in front of us. The horse shied, and both of us men saw the light.

At this point, Daubley asserted, "I did not see double that night, or dream anything either!" Also, he maintained, "I am not a drinking man, nor do I take it as medicine."

Daubley continued, "The bright object just skipped like a sheep runs and suddenly it took a jump and leaped over a tree twenty feet high and disappeared . . . suddenly across the meadow or low land I saw the same thing. It went up into the air twenty or thirty feet and then came down and whirled over the road again . . . the light thing crossed the road and then we heard low singing. It was a strange kind of singing, sadder than you hear at funerals in big churches."

The horse, at this point, was comforted by Schmeck, who stepped cautiously from the buggy and placed a handerchief over its eyes.

"The singing came a little louder, but I could not make out the words," Daubly said. "I own up that for once in my life, I was scared."

Daubley's "scare" probably turned into horror as the bright object slowly took the shape and form of a young girl!

"It had long hair, and was dressed all in white. The arms were bare, and with one of them extended, it pointed toward the black woods over the canal. Then I heard these words come from her: 'They dragged me down . . . they dragged me down . . . my poor life was robbed . . . robbed when they murdered me.'"

The horse-buyer's story continues, "Suddenly it shot into the air, circling the trees, moaning, 'I come . . . I come . . the hour is here.' The last word she fairly shrieked, which caused the horse to raise on his haunches, and the hired man fell onto his back in the dirt. I could see the figure shoot off into the black night, and in a minute it was gone."

As the apparition disappeared into the night sky, the two horrified travellers continued along the road. The horse was calmed, but would not go faster than a slow walk.

"We had not gone far before the animal gave a snort and reared again. I did not see anythng but I knew the horse did. My hired man (Schmeck) jumped out and held him at bridle. I looked ahead and about a quarter of a mile I saw a bluish white light roll around on the top of the fence on the left side."

Daubley had had enough! "I then got mad as the d----." (It is interesting to note that the word, "devil," was not printed in the 19th century newspaper account). "I just felt brave enough to meet fifty spooks and I jumped out of the wagon and went to the side of the fence. I made up my mind to see what the thing was. The bright light came along at good speed but when a sudden spurt of wind blew, the light floated away . . . on came the light again, and suddenly it stretched! It was not a ball but the form of a man with black hair, and it had on a white shirt, nothing more. I'll swear that it was nothing but that, because I saw it. It came right up to me. I stooped down until it got right above me. I then jumped to grab it. Quick as thought itself I fell into a mud puddle. The strange thing was also singing something. I was all mixed up and excited."

Daubley said he gathered his senses, got up, and was treated to even more. "I looked over the field and saw two bright lights floating about in a circle — both the spirits we had seen. One was a man and the other was a woman, who started chasing the man . . . then the two forms floated over above the ruins of a stone house in the field. The northern gable end was standing, and upon the peak of this they sat, and we heard them singing. All of a sudden, everything was black again and we could see no more."

So ends the incredible account of Messrs. Daubley and Schmeck. Two men who swore to the sightings of two ghosts.

Many of the facts surrounding the murder of Adaline Baver, the strange encounter of Daubley and Schmeck, and another recorded murder at a spot not far from where Adaline's body was found have been shrouded by time. But perhaps Miss Baver and another victim did indeed return nearly a third of a century later to visit the land which claimed them in a deathless sleep. Perhaps their spirits remain earthbound and still haunt this part of the county. Perhaps someone played a prank on the two unsuspecting gentlemen. Perhaps imagination inspired the account of James Daubley. Nonetheless, the story remains a bizarre chapter in the ghostly chronicles of Berks County. And the experience was deeply etched in the mind of Daubley, who adds this post script: "It was the worst night of my life. I am fifty years old and don't believe in spooks, but if I live a hundred years I won't forget what happened."

THE PHANTOM OF FIVE LOCKS

— Personal Interviews
October 1981

Even if there were no tales of supernatural happenings at the Five Locks of the Schuylkill Canal south of Hamburg, the locale would lend itself to spectral accounts or canal legends.

A thick, green muck floats as a rug atop stagnant waters within the chambers of the locks, stepping down between a straight, lonely gravel road and a steep cliff rising on the east. The wooded area stretches westward to the Schuylkill River, and is pockmarked with litter and household leavings cast away by unthinking mortals. The canal's once threadbare towpath is a mound of trees, barely discernible and hardly recognizable as a pathway for the barge-tugging mules a century ago.

The canal's lore ranges from the romantic to the ribald. Remote and lonely even today, the remnants of this once-bustling waterway conjure up both history and mystery. Just a scant distance south of Five Locks, the ghost of Adaline Baver rose from the muddy canal banks to cavort near Mohrsville.

The haunting at Five Locks is variously attributed to several sets of circumstances. But each features as its central character a lock-tender and his daughter. And, while the stories' "raison d'etre" may be to fuel the fires of romances which blossom along the dark roadside at Five Locks, they warrant re-telling.

Many canal boatmen were known for their rowdy lifestyle, and canalside mothers would bar the doors and hide the ladies when certain barge and packet crewmen would be in the area.

Enter the lock-tender's daughter in story number one.

It's a variation of a familiar theme. The daughter would meet the canal boat crewman. Their occasional meetings would grow into a budding romance — a romance which would never be fulfilled. The girl's father refused to allow his daughter to see the young man who won her heart. It is likely the lock-tender frowned on his daughter becoming just another girl in just another port, so to speak. The father's anger became rage. He forbade his daughter to ever see the boatman again, and would actually restrain the girl inside the tender's house when he knew her sailing suitor was bound her way.

Disconsolate, the girl plotted her final rendezvous — not with her chosen beau but with her chosen fate. The fear of and hostility toward her father and the emptiness of a stifled young love led her one dismal night to the wall of the deep canal lock chamber. If she could not be with the boy she loved, she would cast her body into the waters which brought him to her. She leaped into the lock — a non-swimmer who would struggle briefly, sink to the bottom and rise again as a corpse.

And rise again . . . as a ghost!

The second version of our tale features the lock-tender and his daughter, but lacks much of the drama and romance of the first. However, the timing and nature of this story makes it equally intriguing.

The simple story was related by the man who brought the long-vacant lock-tender's house from a state of near ruin to quaint and imaginative liveability.

It was Halloween — a long time ago. It was a time when All Saints Day was a time for goblins, ghosts, parties and revelry. The setting of the canalside a century ago obviously presented an ominous backdrop for spooky hijinx. And, the playful young lady who lived in the tender's home would seize the opportunity to play good-natured pranks on the young'uns thereabouts. Dressed in ghostly garb, she chased her young "victims" through the darkness, providing them with contrived terror. But her "trick" was to result in all-too-real terror for the children, and an untimely death for the lock-tender's daughter. Cavorting too close to the edge of the lock chamber and encumbered with her costume, the young woman accidentally stumbled into the water.

The two stories dovetail into our "Phantom of Five Locks" legend. The ghost there is popular fodder for conversation when conversation in Northern Berks County turns to the supernatural. The vision of a young woman has been reported hovering over the water of Five Locks, and the stories have been passed on through the years. One account not only mentions the visual aspect, but also a peculiar noise connected with the spirit. It's been said that, on no particular schedule, the plaintive sound of a splash, followed by muffled cries for help can be heard from the towpath. And, the spectre of a young girl has been seen walking along the edge of the canal bed. On a midnight walk, the girl can be seen slowly turning her sorrowful head northward and then south — perhaps keeping vigil for one more rendezvous with her true, and lost, love.

THE MYSTERIOUS LIGHTS OF "THE BOSHTARD"

— Personal Interview and
Historical Research
December, 1981

The house lies at the end of a narrow, tree-lined roadway leading from a winding country road on the eastern fringe of Reading's suburbs.

It is an imposing structure, surrounded by a wooded area which belies the locale. Within minutes is the bustling Exeter Township commercial area, and the glow of the city sprawl a few miles to the west filters eerily through the night-darkened treescape. It may be said that the place provides a tantalizing setting for a tale of haunting. And, the tales of haunting at this home, or more properly the land around it, have been passed on through several generations.

Let us begin our story with some historical perspectives.

Hundreds of years ago, a rift between the Roman Catholics and Protestants of France resulted in an edict ordering the liquidation of all

Protestants in that country. Many of these Protestants followed the teachings of Besancon Hugues, a German-Swiss reformer. These people became known as "Huguenots," and faced with expulsion or execution in their native land, many fled to neighboring countries.

One of these families were the LeVans. Family records indicate Daniel and Marie Beau LeVan, with five sons and one daughter, emigrated to Holland. Later, five of the children made their way to America. By the mid eighteenth century, the LeVans settled in what is now Berks County. The family grew and prospered, and branched out through the generations and across the developing county, state and nation. Through the years, the LeVans of Exeter and Oley Townships built several magnificent homes on farms which spread from the Oley Valley to the Schuylkill River.

The most recent keeper of the LeVan family flame was Margaret LeVan Brumbach. And, in an effort befitting her wisdom and concern for the proud heritage of the family, Margaret published her genealogical research and colorful memories in book form. It is from this publication that we draw much of what is to follow.

I trust at this point you'll recall the scenario in the opening paragraphs of this story. Now, delete the "suburban fringe," "city glow," and "bustling commercial area" references. Picture the same beautiful, old stone farm house along the same narrow lane, under night skies of a century ago — ever so much darker — in a then-rural area ever so much lonelier and remote.

But more importantly, picture a time before video games, radio or movie theatres. A time when the imagination is fired by the slightest spark of "spooky" stories. It is a Currier and Ives time, bundled-up children huddled near a crackling fire on a night illuminated by a golf ball moon and caressed by a steady breeze whistling quietly through leafless trees.

The farms of several descendants of the original Berks County LeVans were the scenes of many alleged hauntings over the years. Perhaps the stories told and re-told were simply fodder for homespun entertainment. Or, perhaps the stories had a basis in truth. Whatever, the same tales are related to the present generation, and recorded for posterity in the writings of Margaret LeVan Brumbach:

There were tales of two-headed calves or huge dogs — rappings upon the door of the house leading to the inside of the house and upon opening for entrance — nothing! Nothing there but the impenetrable darkness of a moonless night.

Then there would be numberless times the huge house dog, lying at our feet in the long dark evenings lighted by coal oil lamps, many times jumping to our feet because of the dog's savage growls. No investigation ever revealed any plausible cause for these episodes, yet it always left one with the uncomfortable feeling (quoting now from Shakespeare) that there are more things in Heaven and Earth, Horatio, than are dreamed of in your philosophy.

Perhaps the most durable tale of the supernatural eminates from the aforementioned farm house in the forest. Even today, young and old folks visiting the place are treated with the story of the mysterious lights of the "Boshtard."

"Boshtard" was the common name for a soggy meadow lying between the main house and a spring house a few yards away. And, the roots of the "mysterious lights" account go back to the night before the funeral of a LeVan family member several years ago.

As the family prepared for the somber day ahead, there was a need for the "funeral meats" for those who would be coming a distance to attend. Hired help worked to make the necessary arrangements, and the products of their kitchen labors were transported from the main house to the spring house as the glow of sunset filtered through the trees. As darkness gripped the farmstead, a series of torches or flares was put into place to provide light for those transferring the food from kitchen to storage in the springhouse. Thus, the "boshtard" was flushed with a flickering luminosity.

As the story goes, one of the helpers, no discernible reason, suddenly interrupted the evening's toils and leaped upon a back porch wall. Then, in a thick Pennsylvania Dutch accent, the gent called into the torch-punctuated darkness to an unseen phantom: "Du, Johannes Bechtel, Du! If you have a rum bottle come up here and give us a dram!" The bizarre harkening of the spirit of the man who would be buried the next day failed to produce any bottle or rum or, in that case, any ghost. But it did draw a — no pun intended — "spirited" response from those in attendance. Imaginations ran wild. Spurred by the moribund events of the recent past and immediate future, the family members and helpers were easily convinced that the lights brightening the way to the spring house were moving. Bobbing up and down, back and forth, the lights seemed to rush toward them. A suggestion by someone that the mysterious lights had drifted onto the porch resulted in shrieks of fear and utter confusion — not to mention the spillage of many wicker baskets of the "funeral meats."

The story does not necessarily end here. The mysterious lights of the "Boshtard" have supposedly been seen at other times between the funeral of Johannes Bechtel and today. And, there have been reports of other supernatural events at the old LeVan home in Exeter Township. A current resident does not discount the stories of the mysterious lights, nor does she offer any firm evidence or reports of recent sightings. But again, the story does not end here, either.

In the company of her husband and several children, the woman told me of the "haunting" of the old house. But it is not that marked by bobbing and weaving lights of the Boshtard. It is not that of Johannes Bechtel. The woman tells of nocturnal footfalls on a main stairway leading from the foyer to the second floor. She tells of a strange scratching sound on the front door leading to the foyer. She believes she knows what spirit is providing these audible displays. She thinks it is that of a dearly beloved, departed family member — a long-dead family dog.

25

GHOSTS IN THE COUNTRYSIDE

— Personal research

In an unremarkable farmhouse on Basket Road overlooking the picturesque Oley Valley, we find a most extraordinary story. It is told by a prominent Reading banker, and involves the house, his mother, and a most clamorous phantasm.

Strangely enough, this ghost would usually become most active in the fall. It is not often that we find a seasonal specter! One evening, the banker's mother was sitting in her living room quietly going about her business when a rather loud thump was heard on the second floor. The woman gave a start, dropped what she was doing and listened attentively. Seconds after the thump, a rumble was heard. It all came from the top of the stairs and apparently descended with a most thunderous rustle.

This happened many times. Unexplained noises were heard on the second floor and the rumble on the steps persisted. One night, the woman was entertaining neighbors when the uninvited guest made its presence known. The ghostly thump was heard on the stairs. Then, to everyone's shock, a grotesque scream echoed through the house. Then, a flurry of footsteps down the steps. A door at the foot of the steps opened and slammed shut. A loud thump outside. Within seconds, the show was over. The mortal occupants of the living room gazed at each other in disbelief. They had all heard the unearthly chain of events!

Things got so bad that the suspicions of "ghosts" coupled with neighborhood gossip affected the property value of the house. After the woman moved out, a businessman bought the home and the land around it. He had heard about the noisy guest and, to avoid all further aggravation, planned to demolish the "haunted house" and use the property for future development — sans ghosts!

After investigation, it was found that a previous owner of the old house had committed suicide in the dwelling. He had cut either his throat or wrists (past records are vague), and after making the fatal slash ran from an upstairs room, down the steps, and out the front door in a dying terror. Today, he recreates this act to the shock and horror of mortal man!

In other sections of this 864-square mile county, stories have been told and retold over the years. Many defy the imagination and evade any plausible explanation. And, many are more anecdotal than epic in proportion. So, we shall review some of them in the following paragraphs.

In Perry Township there have been rather weird sightings that some of the older folks thereabouts swear to be true. One afternoon, in the sprngtime, a group of farmers gathered around a barn. Their day was nearly done and the sun was midway through its downhill journey.

As they stood around chewing the fat and their Mail Pouch, one man nervously gazed into a field nearby. His pallid complexion and glassy eyes made him look like he'd seen a ghost. He had!

There in the field, several horses ran about. Nothing unusual, you say? Well, these horses were not of the "Trigger" or "Whirlaway" sort — they had no heads!

The headless horses stood in the field, with a strange radiance about them. Each man clearly saw the apparitions, and still today swears to their validity. Who are we to doubt them?

In a house near Belleman's Church, Bern Township, a family was beleaguered by a noisy spirit similar to the one previously discussed in this chapter.

It is documented that a woman had shot her son, and herself, in the old house. For months, nothing had disturbed the tranquility of the family now residing in it. Nothing, that is, until that one fateful day.

The Mrs. of the family was working in the kitchen when she heard the patented rumble of steps on her stairwell. On selected days and nights, the footsteps recurred. Relatives and friends of the family also heard the steps, which could not be explained.

The tenacious footfall held such an emotional grip on the residents of the house that they soon formulated plans for moving. After days of trying to find another home, and continuing to hear the peculiar pitter-patter on the steps, they finally prepared for the big move.

On their moving day, however, things were not quite normal. No, that day, the spirit of the steps was to make its attendance well known. As neighbors, friends and relatives gathered to lend helping hands in the moving chore, they were all treated to an unearthly manifestation.

The moving day was to relieve the tension of the family and rid their minds and ears of the noisy spook. But it seems that the goblin had planned a little going away party for the wraith-weary residents.

The steps came once again, and for the last time. This time they came with such a racket that the entire moving party stood aghast. "It sounded like all hell broke loose," said one ear-witness to the happening. Maybe it did!

From the Hamburg area comes a story about a very unusual gun. The weapon in question had been handed down from generation to generation, but with its present owner, a legend began to take shape.

Somewhere in a past generation, the gun is said to have fatally injured a member of the family that still possesses it. Since that apparent accident, the gun had gone virtually unused. The current owner, however, decided to bring it back into use.

27

After cleaning, polishing and servicing the rifle, it was ready for firing tests. On the range, the gun performed with excellence. Targets were riddled with bullet holes on or near the bullseye. For all intents and purposes, the gun was ready for the supreme test in the forests and fields.

But, to the utter disappointment and disbelief of the marksman, the gun failed its final exam. Despite its accuracy with targets, claybirds and tin cans, the gun quite amazingly would not kill — again. In fact, its owner claimed to actually see the bullets drop suddenly before they were to hit their mark!

After too many frustrating hunting trips, the owner decided to have the gun checked out — by a powwower!

The powwow doctor lived in a farmhouse in central Berks County. His farm typified those of Pennsylvania "Dutch" tradition. Lanky pedicles of corn mustered in acres of fertile topsoil like a giant golden-helmeted army bracing for an early autumn massacre. Stout cattle grazed endlessly on green pasturage hemmed by thistled wire gently enforced with electricity. The farmer, replete with faded coveralls with rolled cuffs, a threadbare baseball cap and calloused hands, similarly exemplified his rugged stock.

Being a powwow doctor did not alienate the farmer from his neighbors. In fact, he had a substantial clientele and his powers were not feared, but moreso used to their fullest advantages by those in need.

In need at this particular time was our friend with the queer shottin' iron. So, he came to the old man for advice, and possibly a powwow cure for the gun's inadequacies.

He conjured up a cure all right, one just as odd as the gun's inability to kill in the hunt. The farmer suggested that the gun's owner urinate down the barrel of the weapon and await evaporation. After this "medication" was applied, the powwower said, the gun would once again function as expected.

To make a long story short, and to circumvent the unpleasant details of the actual treatment, let us simply say that the nimrod took the "doctor's" advice and, amazingly, the gun performed with excellence on his next hunting safari through the wilds of beautiful — and mysterious — Berks County.

A BELIEVER IN BERNVILLE

— Anonymous caller on WEEU's
"Feedback" Talk Show
October, 1981.

She loved to, as she said, "walk over cemeteries."

And, secure with the memories of years spent simply wandering through graveyards, the woman believed the beautiful Sunday afternoon to be no different from so many others. Alone, or with friends or family members she'd silently walk between ancient tommbstones and modern monuments — seeking genealogical facts or simply immersing herself in the quiet, lush landscape punctuated by the morbid markers and colorful floral tributes.

But this day was to bring with it an event which woud linger with the woman for the rest of her life — and convert her into a "believer" in ghosts!

The borough of Bernville has within its borders a pair of adjacent cemeteries. This story embraces both, but begins in the Haag Cemetery, on the eastern fringe of town.

The cemeteries are not, in themselves, particularly engrossing. A narrow macadam road divides the two, and the gnarled roots of trees bordering the Haag Cemetery provides an eerie frame for the amply-shaded yard. Dominating the skyline of the Haag Cemetery is the tall monument to Civil War soldier George D. Fahrenbach, who lived from 1846 to 1919. This striking full-scale statue stands eternal watch over the graves of Haag, and becomes the focal point of our story.

"I love to walk over cemeteries," she recounted, "and this Sunday afternoon was so clear and blue. I said to my grandson 'we're not alone in this cemetery.' He said he didn't see anybody. I said, 'Yes, I do!'"

The woman's memory was keen as she peeled away more than two decades of thought to reveal her tale.

"We were standing near the George Fahrenbach monument. There was the figure of a woman . . . she had on a gray dress and a bonnet and was sort of picking up grass. I told my grandson again, 'we are not alone, there's a lady —.'

"And looking up, just on the spur of the moment, this thing was gone! And then, I looked toward the gate to get on the other cemetery — and there it was! I was thinking to myself, now what could this be?"

The woman tried to reckon with herself — to analyze what had happened. She did not recognize the figure, but swore to herself that, as she says, "I saw that thing as clear as daylight."

The story does not end with her singular experience that clear and blue Sunday afternoon. Her belief was reinforced, then as now, by a relative.

"Several Sundays later, I was up home — my parents lived in the Kempton area — and my father's cousin was there. I related the story to him and he said I was not alone, some more people have seen that thing!"

The old woman's voice is firm, yet cautious as she relates the story today. As unshaken as her vivid memory is her belief in, or at least her acceptance of, ghosts.

She will tell her tale to anyone who shows a desire to listen and absorb it. She continues to walk quietly through cemeteries, seeking and finding whatever solace it provides. She took her sister to the site of her experience, telling her, "This is where I saw that figure of a woman . . . and it disappeared like the turn of a hand."

"I must believe that there are ghosts," she says. "But you don't always get scared about them. I didn't. I didn't have time to get scared."

Surely the woman's encounter with this spectre was brief. Perhaps the figure was that of a departed soul making a phantasmal visit. Perhaps, like the woman telling the story, she simply "loves to walk over cemeteries."

"FEEDING THE DEAD"
AND THE
LEGEND OF THE HONEY POT . . .

— Indian Legends

Christel Neucommer was a farmer in Bethel Township, near the ridge of the Blue Mountains, the hunting grounds of the Indians who had been driven into the hills from the lowlands. The early settlers of the great Schuylkill and Tulpehocken basins had made the hills of northern Berks the last vestige of freedom for the redmen.

Neucommer was awakened one night by the unearthly howling of dogs outside his home. He picked up his rifle and proceeded outside to investigate whatever had disturbed his slumber. Glancing into a field behind his house, he saw a waving line hovering over the grave of his mother. The line materialized into an Indian, who was promptly shot by the disturbed dozer. Neucommer then went to the grave and found a pot of honey. The Indian, according to tradition, was "feeding the dead." It was believed to be a common custom of the Lenni Lenape, but unheard of in white civilization.

Coincidentally (?) days later, Neucommer's wife and children were brutally murdered by Indians.

Another story dealing with this practice has been passed down through the ages. It involves a beautiful young girl, Mary Cavalcasalle. She lived on a farm in northern Berks, near present-day Shartlesville. Described as an "unusually lovely girl, with flowing hair," Mary was the daughter of Huguenot parents who chose the county as their American home.

Her parents had gone away one fateful night, leaving Mary alone with her brother on the farmstead. The parents were to return the following day, after a visit to a distant relative. They were to return to a horror that would dwell with the family for the rest of their lives.

As Mary prepared for bed, she checked the house, tucked her brother into bed and doused the candles. She found her way to her room and drifted into slumber. As she lay there, in that strange void between awareness and sleep, she heard rustling in the adjacent orchard. She knew that wolves and wild cats were prevalent in the Blue Mountains, and wanted to take no chances. She reached for a musket, which was in the corner of the room, crawled to the window facing the orchard and gazed into the moonlit fields. In a cornfield next to the orchard, she thought she saw something move. She took aim with the gun and fired into the field. The rustling ceased and the bestial intruder had been driven away.

The next day, her five-year old brother, Dixon, ran into the home from the field in which he was playing to tell Mary that there was an Indian lying in the cornfield, dying. He was in a pool of blood, his life slowly draining from his body.

Mary was horrified. All too well, she remembered the incident of the previous night, and ran to the field to a sight that would haunt her until her last day.

As she approached the man, she saw that he was just barely alive. He desperately tried to speak, but the warmth of life was rapidly oozing away. Finally, with a superhuman effort, he spoke: "Why did you shoot me, beautiful young lady?" He continued, painfully, "I only came here to place some honey on my mother's grave, who is buried in yonder orchard. It is the fifteenth anniversary of her death."

Mary's heart was broken. She had shot an innocent man, on a mission of love. As she wept by his side, the Indian passed away. Mary's eyes were affixed in tears, and grief filled her young body.

That afternoon, Mary's parents returned to the homestead to find their daughter in a state of severe shock. She woefully told them her dreadful tale. Her father buried the Indian that evening, but the interment failed to inhume the memory.

For the rest of her days, she lived in extreme sorrow. Her eyes reflected her distress, and they say she literally never smiled. Her parents consulted doctors in nearby towns, and powwowers in Oley and Reading. Through these men, they found that a change of scene would be the best medicine. Thus, they travelled west to a new home and a new life for Mary Cavalcasalle. But the memory lingered forever in Mary's troubled mind. Nothing could ever release her from the depths of her misery.

Author Henry W. Shoemaker, in a 1924 book, said, "Those who have the psychic sight perchance may see the Indians on the anniversary, in the dead calm of a summer night, the son handing the mother a pot of honey, the token of the end of his earthly existence. As for Mary Cavalcasalle, let us hope her repentant spirit found lasting contentment and haunts no earthly scenes."

THREE COPPER NAILS

—Personal Interview
January, 1982

Our next story takes us to a small home in one of the crossroads villages of Exeter Township. And, while the weird sounds and scenes

31

of the ghostly encounter took place in the 1960's and came to an abrupt end in a most remarkable way, the source of the spiritual show dates back far before this time.

The actual happenings inside the house are now just titillating memories as the owner of the place recalls events of more than two decades ago. But so vivid are these memories that, still today, they raise the hackles of the family subjected to what went on for those few frightening months.

As a child, the woman remembers the story of the across-the-street neighbor lady dying inside her home, and remembers hushed backyard gossip about the nature of the death. Was it a tragic suicide? No matter — the neighborhood rumor mill, fueled by sketchy reports from authorities and afflicted family members, placed the death in the "mysterious" file and whispered about it for many weeks.

Little did the young girl dream that someday she and her husband would be living inside the house of the "mysterious death." But, in the early 60s, the couple called the place home. And, the recollection of what actually happened, or may have happened inside the home so many years ago, may have enhanced the account which follows, but it becomes very clear that what began to occur in the house took on more than merely imaginational proportions.

As the couple settled in, all was well inside the tiny home. Even the memory of the woman's death inside was seldom brought to mind. But, as the family grew, so did the home. And, as we hear in so many accounts of poltergeistic and ghostly meetings, when the renovations and expansion began, the spirits came out to play. "We'd hear noises," our storyteller relates, "but we thought it was just nothing, just loose boards, nails dropping, whatever."

But soon, loud bangs . . . pictures falling off walls . . . scraping, scratching noises of all sorts. The first target of blame by Mom was, of course, the children. But, after some scolding and confusing feelings of guilt, the children were absolved. The family, en masse, would hear the noises. The kids no doubt raised eyebrows toward Mom as their innocence was proven by whoever or whatever was out there!

Just what was out there? And where? That was the rub. Although most of the noises seemed to come from the attic, soon they were to be heard from nearly every wall and corner of the place. The audible antics of the spooks were soon joined by more physical, if not violent acts.

"One night, Dad heard a real loud bang which awoke everyone," recalls one of the daughters now in her late 20s. "Dad got up to investigate, and there it was — a little stool we kept in the bathroom, laying on the floor in the hallway. We were all asleep — there was really no explanation for that!"

Mom remembers the spirit seemed to have a fondness for wall hangings: "Pictures would bang against the walls and move right in front of our eyes. President John F. Kennedy's picture, after he was assassinated, banged against the wall and turned crooked. And then, after my grandfather died and they divided up the estate, we had this one favorite picture of him hanging in the living room and all of a sudden right in front of all of us it banged three times against the wall and turned and hung crooked!"

The family started to question its own sanity. Perhaps all of this was the product of a simple kind of group hysteria. Perhaps they needed some time away from the place. So, that's exactly what they chose — a vacation far, far away from the home. They were to find, however, that what they left behind would still be there waiting for them when they returned. And, when they returned, they were greeted by someone who at once doused their suspicion of mass insanity and rekindled the fires of fear. While the family vacationed, another relative tended the homestead. He was quick to tell them about his experiences while they were gone. As an anxious family listened, the gent told of noises . . . bumps and thumps . . . lights going on and off . . . items apparently moving by themselves. He wanted no part of the place. And, he had no knowledge of any of the family's previous experiences — they were too embarrassed to ever tell him, or for that matter, anyone else!

Their tale was shared once with a young woman who visited the home with a relative, and immediately commented that she felt the "presence" of "something or someone" inside the house. But other than a very select few close friends, the family members have been hesitant to tell their stories, until now.

The spooks staged a "welcome home" party for the family upon their return from vacation, as the strange sounds and events continued. One incident still mystifies them. One night a caged bird in a hallway began to flop around strangely, in a way never before witnessed by anyone in the house. They watched quizically as the two family dogs and a cat ran into the hallway and joined the crazed bird, in a kind of bestial cringe caused by an unseen force.

But, over and above all others, one Friday night's experience was enough to cause the mother of the family to seek some kind of help. "I was in the one room sewing," she says, "and I looked up from the sewing table and all of a sudden, our cellar door opened — you know, just slowly — not like a draft coming through — it just slowly creaked open. Well, I just stood up there, riveted in the spot, and I looked and the cat was on the chair in the living room and it leaped up and ran out to the front door. I couldn't even move. And while I was standing there, the cellar door just slowly — it seemed like an eternity — creaked closed again." The woman ran out of the house in fear, to a neighbor's home.

Through one of the sons of the family, the word got out about some of the strange happenings inside the house. And, one fellow at the young man's place of employment said he could help.

He said he knew of a powwow doctor who could exorcise the spirit from the home. The "doctor" would have to know the facts, and the family would have to believe that he could rid them of their annoying wraith. It was agreed.

33

At a predescribed time, the folks inside the house were to drive three copper nails into the attic door, while the powwower, at precisely the same time, would read an appropriate verse from one of the powwowers' "mannuals," the "Sixth and Seventh Books of Moses." As strange as it seemed at the time, one of the family members performed the deed, using nails provided by the powwower, while "doc" did his part on his end.

It worked.

Suffice to say, the family from that moment on, saw nothing, heard nothing and had no trouble with the noisy inhabitant. Now, you may ask, is that it? Could the story have ended that simply and effectively? Well, you should know better! You should have come to expect anything but a simple remedy for such a haunting.

But, alas, we cannot provide anything more. The powwower's "treatment" was apparently the cure for what ailed the family for those months. The three copper nails were driven into the attic door and still today remain firmly embedded in the door, representing either silent sentries guarding whatever is imprisoned within the walls of the house, or monuments to whatever was sent fleeing by the powwower.

THE GHOSTS OF THE OPERA HOUSE

— Research, 1971-1982

Many tales of the supernatural have their origins amid the rubble of lives cut short by untimely, unnatural or unexplained death. And, while many theories of existence on "the other side" discount these prerequisites, they continue to be part and parcel to a good number of "ghost stories."

This particular story begins with the most tragic and calamitous event in Berks County history. Let us set the stage with the account appearing in the Tuesday, January 14, 1908 issue of the Reading HERALD.

Death by fire in its most horrible form burst upon Boyertown last night. Over the Opera House, crowded with the flower of Boyertown's residents, swept a very hell of flame, gutting the building and carrying over 150 souls into eternity . . . it was too appalling for words. At one moment the happy, innocent folk sat watching the gay pageantry on stage before them . . . the next instant the hoarse cry of agony . . . and the futile endeavor to snatch one's self and one's dear ones from death in its most grisly, ghastly form.

And so, while reading like the introduction of a Gothic novel, the article simply attempted to put into words the stark reality of the Rhoads Opera House fire of 1908.

"Opera House" may have been somewhat of a grandiose misnomer. The hall could commfortably accommodate about three hundred people, and was situated on the second floor of a building which housed the Farmers National Bank at ground level. In retrospect, it seems obvious that the room's size, location and ways of ingress and egress made it pitifully and eventually tragically, unsuited for auditorium use. There were fire escapes, but poorly marked and accessible only through windows. The width of the main doorway was only 46½ inches, and the door opened inward at the base of a steep and narrow staircase. And still, the building's owner, a Doctor Rhoads, maintained that the building was fine for public use — even after 170 men, women and children had suffocated, or had been trampled or incinerated at a Sunday School benefit play.

Response from the community was gratifying for the organizers of the show scheduled for that fateful Monday, January 13. Three-hundred twenty tickets were sold for the semi-religious play, "The Scottish Reformation." Proceeds from the event would go to St. John's Lutheran Church of Boyertown. But those proceeds, as well as 170 human lives including the young daughter of the church's pastor, Rev. A. M. Weber, would go up in the smoke of tragedy that night.

Harriet Monroe was director of the play on that cold night, and the services of Henry Fisher were summoned to operate a stereopticon to achieve certain desired effects.

The gaiety of the evening was to be cut short ever so suddenly. So suddenly, in fact, that the exact cause of the fire is still a matter of debate. The sweep of the fire that night was so swift that no one knows for sure where the fire started. Some say the "magic lantern" of Mr. Fisher. Or a hydrogen tank explosion from a calcium light. Or coal oil footlights kicked over by a performer, igniting the curtain. Daniel Schlegel, a survivor, mnaged to escape through one of the ill-conceived fire escapes: "I saw exactly how the fire started. It did not start at the stage at all, but near the rear door.

"There was a noise like an explosion and every one ran for the door. When a large crowd was gathered at the door there was a second explosion and they were all enveloped in a large mass of flame.

"This caused a stampede, and it was not until then that the lights upset in the front of the building. All of the people then became excited as they saw fire on both sides of them. There was fire at both ends of the hall, but there was none in the center."

The Reading HERALD said that after the Rhoads Opera House fire, ". . . all other tragedies in Berks County pale into insignificance."

Macabre descriptions of the tragedy colored the pages of newspapers across America. Tales of the "smells of roast flesh" and of the entire families lost in the blaze. The fire became somewhat of a "media event" in 1908 as major papers sent reporters to cover the holocaust and its resultant impact on this small Berks County town.

The fire claimed several notables: former Boyertown burgess Henry Binder, former Senator Dr. Frank Brunner, and Daniel Gable, a foreman at the Boyertown Burial Casket Company.

More than a score of bodies were never claimed, and many more were rendered unidentifiable by the intense blaze. In the cleanup process following the darkest night in the county's history, loose bones and body parts were collected and placed in a separate coffin which would join others in a common grave on the sloping hillside of Fairview Cemetery. Another morbid account confirms that the ashes of the building itself were buried, as they were thought to contain a good amount of human ashes.

As undertakers, nurses and police officers arrived from neighboring towns and cities, the borough was placed under martial law by Burgess Kohler. Police maintained tight security at the ruins overnight, fending off looters and ghoulish sightseers until the morning sun would bring light upon the grisly scene.

As the dawn broke, flags flew half-mast in the grief-stricken town. Aid came from a wide radius — money, clothing, medical — and the town wiped its eyes to start anew.

With more than 150 gravediggers standing by to bury the dead, the stories of the event began to take shape. Fact and rumor, suspicion and superstition all played roles in the ensuing, seemingly never-ending unraveling of the details of the tragedy.

While not an integral part of our "ghost story," these details merit repeating. There were the entrepreneurs who quickly jumped on the scene. Artist K. B. Kostenbader published 11 x 14 glossy photo-art "souvenirs" of the tragedy. The United Traction Company of Reading was chastised for allegedly overcharging a bereaved relative for transport of his dead family members from Boyertown on the daily trolley run.

Rumors circulated that the blaze was a stunt to cover up a robbery of the bank office below the Opera House. This was quelled quickly. A Coroner's Jury suggested to the District Attorney that the show's director, Mrs. Monroe; the stereopticon operator, Mr. Fisher; and the deputy safety director, Harry McBechtel, should each be charged with criminal negligence for being, in the jury's words, "inexperienced, incompetent and lax."

In a classic case of "closing the barn door after the horse has escaped," the Boyertown fire helped re-shape fire and safety authorities' thinking of fire exits, escapes and appurtinant regulations.

But let us turn our attention from the actual event to the bizarre stories which follow. Or, more properly, with one story which preceded the tragedy of January 13.

Wallace and Paul Gottschall were two young boys who managed to escape from the Opera House inferno that night. But, if their mother had allowed her intuition to govern her actions, they may never have gone to the show: "I was worried all evening and I was sorry that I had allowed my boys to go to the play. I knew something was going to happen. I could feel it in my bones.

"I heard the alarm of fire, and rushed to the front door. There I saw what I had expected. The Opera House was in flames. My two boys were in the building!"

Mrs. Gottschall's quotes in the next day's HERALD are thought-provoking, indeed. But the accounts to follow add even more kindling to the fires of the imagination.

The aura of tragedy in Boyertown that night conjured up many tales of ghostly occurrences, some of which were reported to the following day's papers.

State and local police called in to guard the borough while under martial law reported numerous unnatural experiences. One young woman pleaded for police help, saying she was haunted by the spirits of the Opera House dead crying out to her for help. The state troopers offered to watch her home throughout the night of the 13th, but still the woman would open a window every hour to keep a vigil for any ghosts who may appear.

An even more grotesque, yet strangely touching story came, too, from one of the state policemen detailed to guard the ruins of the Opera House, that cold, dark night. Once again, we shall let the Reading HERALD tell the story:

A man in his night shirt was found at 12:30 trying to enter the ruins. He said he was at home sleeping and that his dead wife came to see him. She told him to go to a certain place in the ruins, right where she sat, and that there it would be possible for her to talk to him.

The man, who is an elderly one, has been worrying considerably because he could not identify the body of his helpmate. He sat he is a great believer in ghosts.

It took the combined strength of three state policemen to work him away from the ruins and take him to his home some distance away. He was barefooted on his midnight march and was very cold. A state policeman was detailed to stay with him all night.

What led the mystery man on his "midnight march?" Was it a fanatical love shattered by the sudden disaster? Or was the spirit of his "helpmate" indeed returning to beckon him for a final, melancholy meeting? And would it truly be a "final" meeting?

The building was rebuilt, reinforced and reinhabitated, and today stands in mid-town Boyertown as a reminder of this tragedy, a monument to those who died there, and, perhaps, a rendezvous spot for the spirits which rose from the ashes.

A FAMILY AFFAIR

— *Personal Research*
January, 1982

What if YOU should see a ghost — something you could not explain? Who would you tell? Would you simply keep it to yourself, too embarrassed or perhaps too frightened to share your experience with anyone else?

That is the question you will be faced with when, and if, you are confronted with the situation. And, as we have found in other stories in this volume, there is a sense of comfort when one who has seen the unexplainable is joined by another who has, too, witnessed the same thing.

The cast of characters in this tale includes Donna, who introduces us to her own unexplainable encounter; her husband Bob, who was to share the encounter later; and a host of brothers, sisters, sons, daughters and friends. And, oh yes, some persistent and ubiquitous spirits who made the humans' stay in an old home near Birdsboro quite, shall we say, interesting.

The home is in a row of seven along a hilltop road outside Birdsboro. Its outward appearance gives no hint of mystery. It belies any attachment to being "haunted." But for Donna, Bob and the rest, it would be difficult to deny that it is.

We'll turn the clock back to 1967. Donna and a girlfriend lived in the house, each with a child from a previous marriage. Donna was first to notice that something was awry. "After we had lived there awhile you'd start reading or watching television or something and the next thing you'd be looking around to see if something was in the room with you, because you just felt strange."

The strange feeling was indescribable. Donna fumbles for words to explain. She says it was a strong sense of someone looking over a shoulder, or staring from afar. A shrug of the shoulders and a smile of confusion ends the search for words. "It wasn't an unfriendly feeling, it was just as if someone else was in the room with us."

Donna remarried. Her friend left, and her new husband, Bob, moved in. Settling into the new domestic situation, Donna's uncomfortable sensations were swept away briefly by the pleasure of the new marital arrangement. But soon, the memories of the "strange feelings" were recalled with Bob expressing the same sensation. The uneasiness of the couple was perhaps shared by a Persian cat who lived in the home with them. Often, they recall, the feline would be seen staring into a corner of the room, eyes affixed suspiciously to no visible target, at the precise time one of the human occupants would be flushed with the feeling that someone, or something, was in the room with them.

The house was to become home for two more people when Bob's daughter and Donna's sister came to live with them. Again, there were no discussions on the supernatural feelings experienced by Bob, Donna and the cat. But an unsolicited testimonial from Bob's daughter helped bolster the story. Donna says, "She came down one morning with a confused, if not scared, look on her face. Prior to going to sleep, she had her bedroom lights out, and happened to look up and see a man — or a figure of a man — standing at the foot of her bed! She said he was wearing black trousers, a white shirt, and had his hands on his hips and was looking down at her. And then, she said he silently walked along the side of the bed and just disappeared!"

Donna knew her teenage step-daughter had a vivid imagination, but accepted the story, in respect to the less visible manifestations they had experienced. And, in short order, the girl's startling revelation would be corroborated by yet another character in the continuing story.

Bob's son came to the house while on leave from the Navy, meeting a girlfriend there for a quiet evening with the family. The evening stretched into the early hours of the morning, and the sailor son's friend was invited to spend the night in Bob's daughter's room, left empty while its occupant was visiting an out-of-town friend. You'll remember that the daughter may not have been the ONLY occupant of the eerie bedchamber! Again, the young woman, who was about to spend the night there, had no way of knowing about the previous happenings in the room, and so added substance to the developing ghost story.

At this point, we could almost interject a previous paragraph. "Hey, you've got a strange house here," the young guest said the next morning. Bob and Donna waited for more, with goose-bumps rapidly rising on their skin.

The girl continued, "I must have been dreaming, but I know I was awake. I rolled over, looked up and saw a man standing at the foot of the bed!"

He was wearing dark trousers.

And a white shirt.

And put his hands on his hips.

And walked alongside the bed and vanished into thin air!

But this was not the end of her story.

"After this thing — this man — disappeared, I rubbed my eyes. I looked around and tried to sort things out. But then I heard, real clearly, the sound of a horse and buggy. I remember especially the squeaky buggy seat. I was a little confused, a lot scared, but I managed to calm down and get to sleep."

An anxious Bob and Donna listened, and disclosed the details of the prior uncanny events in the room. And the next day, Bob happened upon a next door neighbor, who was approached with a question: Was there ever anyone in the immediate area who would be driving a horse-drawn wagon at that hour of the day? Not anymore, the neighbor assured him, but many years ago a woman would pilot her buggy past the row of houses, on her way to do business in Birdsboro.

And, the neighbor recalled one particular peculiarity about the now-deceased coachwoman. It was a peculiarity which would be noticed by and would perturb the neighbors when the woman's rides were of the nocturnal sort.

It was a very . . . squeaky . . . buggy seat!

There were more experiences which, to this day, remain as mysteries to all involved. One of those experiences took place as all members of the family settled in for the night. All was quiet throughout the house until Donna was startled by a loud bang which appeared to eminate in the attic. Donna jumped up from the bed, expecting to find comfort in Bob's arms as he, too, reacted to the sudden and disquieting noise. But Donna looked down to see Bob peacefully dozing, undisturbed by a noise Donna recalls could have "awakened the dead."

Unnerved by the interruption, Donna decided to walk downstairs to the kitchen for a midnight cup of juice to calm her nerves. Soon, though, she was joined in the kitchen by her sister.

"Why are you down here?" asked the sister.

"Oh, no reason."

"Donna, well, uh, did you hear something a few minutes ago?"

"Uh, well, what do you mean?"

"You know — a loud bang — like it was coming from the attic?"

"Well, èr, yes. Did you hear . . .?"

"I sure did — scared the heck out of me!"

"What do you think it was?"

"I wish I knew."

"So do I."

This verbal exchange, or something like it, seemed to soothe the jittery women, and substantiate the individual fears of the two.

The sisters continued to sense an uneasiness about the house they shared. Donna would be in a room, start up a conversation with her sister and, in a double-take, notice that her sister wasn't in the room with her! Another time Donna says she actually saw a female figure dressed in a long, lacy gown and a bonnet. Donna fails to remember much from this encounter, however. At the time, she didn't pay much attention, thinking that the figure was her sister, dressed in a "granny gown" style nightgown. From the angle she saw the woman, no face was visible. But again, "Sis" was nowhere to be found, and later confirmed that she wasn't anywhere near that room at the time of Donna's sighting.

Another visitor to the "haunted house" near Birdsboro was treated to a brief but scary meeting with the unknown of the upstairs. Donna tells of the friend who asked to use the bathroom on the second floor, and returned downstairs minutes later with a look of fear on his face. "I'm never going up there again," he said.

"Why?" asked Donna, "what's wrong?"

"I don't know — but there's something really strange up there. When I came out of the bathroom and passed by that one bedroom, I felt something weird!"

The bedroom he passed was the same one used by the two young women who saw the figure of the man by the bed.

Bob and Donna have moved out of the house on the hill. They are still miffed as to who or what may have been with them in their former residence. Donna says simply, "there was unquestionably something in that house — I don't know what it was."

Reflecting on her most frightening encounter with the phantom in the granny gown, Donna asks herself, "Was I sleeping — was I awake? Did it really happen? It seemed so real at the time and it still seems real. I just came to grips with myself and realized, THIS IS A GHOST, and I haven't been afraid of ghosts since! There was no fear . . . the fear of ghosts left me at that time."

Indeed, both Donna and Bob today speak of their years in the house with a kind of detached amusement. Surely, what was so frightening at the time is now a memory — a memory the couple feels has in its strange way, enriched their lives.

THE TALES OF THREE HUNTERS

* **The Wild Man of Northern Berks**
* **A Strange Ball of Light**
* **The Eternal Hunter**

— Dr. Alfred Shoemaker and
Personal Research
March, 1982

As anyone who has ever spent the night in a deep forest knows, the sounds of nature at night can be alarming. The slightest crack of a branch or plaintive wisp of wind through the leves can rip through the darkness like thunder. The cry of a nocturnal creature torments the mind and provides for a restless, if not sleepless night.

Indeed, the forest harbors many sources of mystery and misunderstanding. A precious few of us truly commune with nature, while many of us make occasional token pilgrimages into the wilds, in a noble attempt to pay homage to the wilderness.

Many of Berks County's oldest legends evolve from the forests of early Berks — our portion of Penn's Wood which was dense, unexplored and inhabited by wild beasts and native-Americans, all neatly disposed of by encroaching civilization. Still today, the woodlands of Berks provide their stories, three of which we will examine in this segment.

We credit the first story to noted folklorist and former Historical Society curator Dr. Alfred L. Shoemaker, who in turn credits its origin to Herbert Kauffman of Shartlesville.

With apologies to the "abominable snowman" of Asia and "Bigfoot" of the American northwest, let us now unravel the legend of the "Wild Man of North Berks."

A group of turn-of-the century hunters trekked deep into the woods of the Blue Mountain, north of Shartlesville, in search of the stout, plentiful deer which roamed the hillsides of the county's northern fringe. The men were veterans of many expeditions into the forest, so they were well familiar with the tracks of the denizens of the deep woods. They udoubtedly knew that the mountain was, at one time, home for wolves, mountain lions, bears, lynx and many more species driven to extinction in this area. But one set of footprints they came upon that particular day defied identification and presented a challenge to the sportsmen. And as much as they sought the mysterious prey with large, human-like feet, no quarry could be found.

A few days after this first safari, one of the men decided to return to the same spot to try his luck at locating the strange animal. The hunter positioned himself so he could survey the immediate area, and awaited the arrival of the baffling beast. The sun had set and the forest was changing its scenerio and cast of characters for its twilight show.

Suddenly, the solitude of the evening was disrupted by the rustling of the freshly-fallen autumn leaves. Something was approaching!

"He knew it was not a deer," Dr. Shoemaker writes. "He took aim, but before he could pull the trigger the animal was upon him. From his back it tore his hunting pouch. And in a second the mysterious animal was gone. Then there was silence."

Within days, the man and others returned to the site of the attack, but there was no further activity from within the woods, and no sight of the mystery creature.

"The following spring Henry Fink, while hunting, came to a large spring," Dr. Shoemaker continues. "Heading toward it for a drink of cool water, he spied a strange form in the bushes. It was shaped something like a human being, only it was much, much larger. Frightened, Fink carefully retraced his steps. And once out of sight of the creature, he rushed home."

A later investigation by Fink and some brave friends turned up some footprints similar to, but much larger than a human's. The creature was not seen on the Fink party's second hike into the woods, and has not been reported since. But the story preserved through the years has taken its place as one of the most interesting legends of our own "north woods."

The next story is far removed in time and place from the former. This time: the late 1970's. This place: a forest in Robeson Township near Gibraltar.

For years Randy Moyer stalked these woods, located adjacent to his home. But one year, the tranquility of the silent wait for deer was broken by a sighting which to this day remains a mystery.

Like many other deer hunters, Randy positioned himself at one point where experience taught him his prey was likely to be found. Year after year, he'd quietly listen for a sign — look for the flash of a white tail, and maintain a ritualistic hunter's vigil. The rec room of the Moyer home is adorned with trophies attesting to his prowess with both arrow and bullet.

But one year's sojourn into the neighboring woods will forever register in Randy's memory as the most confusing and confounding encounters of his life.

The day began like most others. The light of dawn filtered through the trees and bathed the underbush — its warmth gradually drinking up the dewdrops and breathing in the thick ground-covering mist.

Randy was enthusiastic. He felt good about the coming day's hunt. He was off to a bright start, and his huntsman's intuition told him his patience would be rewarded.

As the morning matured, the hopes of an early kill began to fade. But the day was to reach a climax within minutes.

Randy gropes for words to describe what happened that day. He apologizes as he explains how his friends scoffed at his story. He questions his own veracity as he recalls the weird experience etched in his brain.

"I really can't explain it," Randy says. "I was just camped out at my usual spot when I saw this . . . this THING in the distance. At first, I didn't know what to make of it. Right from the beginning, as I saw it in the distance, through the trees, it looked like a ball of light. It wasn't a cloud, or a ball of milkweed, or anything like that. I had no idea what it was. But it slowly came toward me — right at me — and weaved between the trees. It kind of glided easily in and out of the trees like it knew what it was doing and where it was going. I just froze up, and couldn't move! In a way, I guess I was fascinated by what I was seeing. But I also guess I was scared as hell!"

"Well, I think I toyed with the idea of blasting whatever it was with my gun, but like I said, I was sort of in awe of whatever the thing was. It was amazing how it just went in and out of the trees."

"And then — now you're not going to believe this — but then it came to within a few yards of me and it stopped. There it was, plain as day, a ball of light — a kind of cloudy light if you know what I mean — just hovering at about eye level over the ground. It was about the size of a basketball, and it had no real features, just a round ball of light."

"Anyway, I stared at it for what seemed to be a few minutes and — POOF — it was gone. It didn't slowly fade away, or disintegrate, or move at all. It was strange, it just popped out of sight!"

Randy says it seemed to position itself opposite him as if it was cognizant and aware that he was there. "I know it was just a ball of light, or something, but it seemed to possess some kind of intelligence. Aw hell, I don't know — I'll never know what it was!"

So, what was it that Randy Moyer saw that day? A rational and intelligent man, he has discounted such suggestions as smoke, moisture, milkweed, gas, or the reflection of light. Little is left with which to attempt to explain this phenomenom. The sighting steps beyond the realm of ghosts perhaps into metaphysics. Or does it? The sense of the supernatural experienced by Randy that morning is best expressed in his frustration: "The thing seemed to want to communicate. I know it sounds crazy, I know I probably sound like I'm some kind of a nut, but I felt that I should have said something to it. And, I felt like it may not have left so quickly and unexplainably if I had tried to talk to it."

These days, Randy still hunts at his favorite spot. He still performs the rituals of man's oldest and basic instinct. But, these days, he keeps a lonely lookout not only for deer, but also for a possible return visit of whatever it was that passed his way that day.

Let us now return to the writings of Dr. Alfred Shoemaker for the legend of the Eternal Hunter, or in the Pennsylvania Dutch dialect, the "Eewich Yeeger."

It is said that on the Yellow Mountain, southwest of Galen Hali, there lived a legendary red fox. The elusive creature had eyes that glowed in the dark and sparks flew from is tail as it pranced across the rocky forest floor. But an old Indian fable promises that whomsoever killed the fox would come upon a fortune of gold.

One night in November, 1811, a cunning hunter decided to test the fox, and swore on a Bible before setting out in search for the animal, that should he not kill the fox, he would ride his chestnut stallion and lead his pack of fox hounds through the hills in a never-ending quest for the fox.

Atop Yellow Mountain, the hunter and his dogs picked up the trail of the fox, and it wasn't long until he spied the strange animal. A shot rang out, but the fox did not fall. Soon, the fox was seen again, along a treacherous rocky ridge on the mountain. The hunter fired again, but in the wink of an eye, an unexpected flash of light and a loud clap of thunder caused the horse to rear up and send its rider down the rock ledge to his death.

He fulfills his solemn promise, and has become the "Eewich Yeeger."

But the story continues. And, a letter sent to Dr. Shoemaker offers an outstanding account of the "Eternal Hunter" and a logical, if not humorous approach to its authenticity.

The writer begins, "My dad and I were skunk hunting about two o'clock in the morning of November 3, 1923. All of a sudden we heard the Eewich Yeeger. He came along the Yellow Mountain ridge. Suddenly he changed his course and headed for our direction. After having heard my grandfather's weird tale of the Eternal Hunter and being a boy of the tender age of 12, you can imagine how I felt. I cannot begin to describe the fright I suffered that night. I shall not forget the incident if I live 200 years. My dad was not the type of man that believed in the supernatural tales, but he admitted in later years that he too felt the cold chills up his spine. But to continue. As the Eewich Yeeger came closer my dad pulled me behind a clump of alder brush. The weird spirit went directly over us with a roar and a whirring of wings.

"We were about 20 or 30 feet from the shore of the lake. And we heard a splash of water, so my dad with his five-cell focusing flashlight threw the beam into the direction of the splash. And to our relief, what we saw there at last made sense: A flock of about 30 Canadian geese, milling and threshing about in the darkness. How, why or where they came from I will never tell you. All I know is I was too weak to walk for quite a few miutes after that. Needless to say, that settled the skunking expedition for that night. We took our skunk dog and made for our 1917 Model T Ford that was parked a mile away and returned home.

"If you doubt that the honking of the flock of Canadian geese does not sound like a pack of hounds baying, next time you see and hear a flock fly by, listen to them. Then use your imagination a bit. Picture yourself as being out in the wee hours of the morning on a cold, damp, foggy night, and recall the tale of the Eewich Yeeger. You will experience some sort of reaction!"

It is said that the plaintive sounds of the Eternal Hunter, his horse and hounds, can still be heard on a damp winter's night on the Yellow Mountain, near the Berks-Lancaster county line.

A GHOST NAMED YOST

— Historical Review Article,
January, 1956

One of the primary ideas generated through religion is that we will all continue to live eternally, beyond our deaths as earthbound mortals. And so, if one is to be truly faithful, one cannot practically deny the existence of spirits. Furthermore, many classic "ghost" stories are deeply rooted in religion, or at least in the faith that our souls shall live on after our bodies expire.

Such is the case in the story of a ghost named Yost. Yost Yoder, to be precise. Yost Yoder of the Oley Valley who departed this life in the mid 18th century, but whose spirit returned dramatically to a daughter years after his death.

For this tale, we turn to folklorist and author John Joseph Stoudt, PhD, who retrieved the story from a 1774 publication entitled, "Verschiedene Alte und Neuer Geschichten von Erscheinungen der Geister." The story is touted as coming from the lips of Elizabeth Yoder, daughter of Yost, who spoke with her father on August 14, 1743, more than two years after he had died!

It is said that Yost was a kind man, and a thoughtful father. But before he could express certain feelings to Elizabeth, he passed away. This strong desire to speak again to his daughter and other children was, however, fulfilled that August morning.

Elizabeth woke with a strange feeling that day. She told her mother that she felt her father was trying to contact her. She described an uncanny fear of sorts, fear that her father was following close behind her. The eerie sensation accompanied her throughout the morning. Unable to explain the feeling, or gain a sympathetic ear from doubting family members, she tried her best to sort out the emotional trauma she was going through.

Elizabeth was overwhelmed by the prospect of chatting with her father. She was driven to put down her chores in the field and yard and return inside the house. She followed this instinct and entered a side room. Her blood surged nervously through her body — she grew tense as she peered toward a bed in the room and had her suspicions confirmed. Sitting on the bedside was Yost Yoder, who had died two years ago.

"What are you doing, my child?" he asked in a friendly, quiet tone.

Elizabeth was shocked. Any amount of emotional preparation she could have made for this moment could not have seen her through the initial encounter. She ran in terror to another room, where she collapsed to the floor in front of her mother. Mrs. Yost was frightened for her daughter's sanity and safety. She packed her off to a neighbor's home for a few days, in hopes that her fears would be allayed and the change of scenery would calm her and remove the thoughts of spiritual contact.

But the absence from her home only made her heart grow fonder for another meeting with her father. Four days later, she ran back home, back to the same side room. And there was her father.

"What are you doing, my child? Where are your brothers?"

"They are not here," she replied, regaining her composure.

(At this point, the story begins to take a novel twist, and we begin to get a hint of the reason it was repeated in its time. I shall explain soon.)

The father-spirit continued: "I left the world so quickly, without speaking to you, but perhaps it is just as well. Now, obey your mother. Do not scorn or despise her. She is on the right road. And when she departs she will go to the right place. And the man: do not despise or scorn him. He is on the right road and preaches the truth."

"Which man?" asked Elizabeth.

"The Frenchman. Tell this to your brothers, your sisters, and all your good friends."

Still puzzled by her father's reference to "the man," Elizabeth nonetheless assured her father that she would obey his instructions. She broke down in tears and asked why he had not returned sooner.

"The time is not yet come. I could not come sooner," he told her.

Elizabeth was told that all was well: "I am at the good place . . . my brother is with me. It goes very well with us." But the spirit then offered some ominous thoughts: "Tell me, why did you run away yesterday? That was unnecessary. I am your dear father; why were you afraid? As you were frightened you shall have to bear severe illness — most severe. Death will approach you three times, you scarcely will survive. If you live, your life shall not be shortened because of it. Now I will depart and never return."

After those terse and frightening words, a most incredible display took place. As a strobe light would flash brightly in the darkness, a flash of black light split the daylight — and the ghost of Yost Yoder disappeared.

46

Now — that "novel twist" I referred to. You'll notice that Yost referred to "the man" in his admonitions to his daughter. "The man . . . preaches the truth . . .," he said. The "FRENCHman," he asserted.

Dr. Stoudt, recounting the Yost Yoder story in a 1956 HISTORI-CAL REVIEW OF BERKS COUNTY article, theorizes that the "French-man" was none other than Dr. George DeBenneville, who came to the Oley Valley a year before the time of this story. It was a time of religious confusion in the area. Dr. Stoudt pointed to the breakdown of the Synods, the lack of credibility of the followers of Matthias Baumann and "raids made by the brothers from Ephrata on the Oley people." He said, quite simply, "the valley was the prey for any religious leader."

Apparently Dr. DeBenneville fashioned himself as a religious leader. He was also, it was recorded, a friend of the printer who published the Yost Yoder account. Dr. Stoudt concludes, "it does not take much historial imagination to suspect that probably the anonym-ous author of this story was DeBenneville, who perceived its value in helping to win converts by use of the bizarre and wonderful."

Perhaps, Dr. Stoudt. But then again . . . .

ALONG THE "HAUNTED HIGHWAY"

— *Personal Research*
January, 1982

There is little reason to travel the winding road from Shoemakers-ville to Berne, one of many roads bypassed by time and relevance. The pathway weaves over and around the Schuylkill River, the overgrown canal bed and the railroad tracks. The house which harbors our next tale is along this "haunted highway" of north-central Berks County.

A few miles to the north, the phantom of Five Locks walks the night. Likewise to the south, the ghost of Adaline Baver roams the canal towpath. In fact, the area just north of Shoemakersville is well-known for its unusual happenings. It is home for more than one "pow wow" doctor. And, the strange story of the "haunted hoedown" still survives today. It is said that in an old one-room schoolhouse some-where along this road, the ghosts come out for an old-fashioned "social." One seasoned citizen up that way tells us he's seen spectral square dancers in shadowy profile, and he's heard a phantom fiddler's eerie strains pierce the solitude of a dark night.

But our story deals not with the ghosts of the schoolhouse or canalside. No, this spirit inhabits a simple farmhouse which is not unlike dozens of others along so many similar roads in the county. And, the human occupants of the home are common folk, with a deep religious faith expressed in numerous icons and hand-made orna-ments which adorn their remodeled home. It is this faith, perhaps, which reinforces their belief in life beyond the grave.

Again, may we note that the home has undergone extensive renovations. This is consistent with a pattern we have noticed running through so many reported ghost stories. And even as Dottie and Bill Strohecker were busily converting the somewhat rundown former home of Bill's grandparents, they would hear strange noises. Simple knocks and creaks within walls were written off as the old building re-settling during re-construction. Tools would disappear and turn up in the most unlikely place later. Each incident was explained away rationally, if not cautiously. That is, until more dramatic manifestations were noticed.

While the home isn't completely remodeled even at this writing, the family has moved inside and has set up housekeeping amid the sawdust and studs. After a while, Dottie and Bill chuckled at their misplacing of tools and the unexplained noises, and blamed any further abnormal occurrences on what they came to call "the ghost." No particular ghost, mind you, just a pesty, generic ghost.

For several weeks, the "ghost" would continue to play tricks on the Stroheckers. But, the couple kept the inside joke from the young, impressionable children. They didn't want to hint that a ghost may actually reside in their home, for fear of the kids' reaction. As it turned out, however, the kids didn't need their parents to introduce them to the spirit world — the spirits invited themselves to theirs!

"Our youngest son was talking in his sleep one night," says Dottie. "I couldn't at first understand him, listening through the wall. But then I could understand him saying, 'Go away . . . go away, please . . . I can't play with you . . . please go away.'" The next morning, Dottie asked her son about the chatter. "I asked him if he remembered talking in his sleep the night before."

"Sure, Mom," said the little boy.

"Who were you talking to?" asked Mom.

"Oh, just the ghost," replied the boy to a dumbfounded mother.

Now the parents' inside joke took on a new dimension and stark realism. A family discussion revealed that all members had had experiences they could not explain. They all suspected ghosts but never before mentioned their suspicions in an open family forum.

The next months were filled with the unexplained. A capable seamstress, Dottie would leave unfinished sewing projects in the bedroom until she found enough time to finish them. As absolutely incredible as it may seem, Dottie swears that the ghost actually finished one of the projects for her.

She says that for several weeks, a jacket needing repairs was left upon a chest at the foot of her bed. One day, she knew, she'd get around to sewing a new zipper in it. Well, one day the zipper was sewn in, but not by Dottie, Bill, or the kids. She claims the new zipper simply appeared in the jacket one morning, sewin in by the ghost!

Sound unbelievable? Well, as they say, you ain't heard nothin' yet!

We'll let Dottie tell it: "I was half asleep — half awake, you know, just kind of dozing off, when I had this dream. I saw two children playing with a simple rag doll. The girl was holding it and cuddling it, but the boy was tormenting the girl. The kids were both dressed in very old-fashioned clothing. Anyway, the boy picked up a stick which was hot and charred black on one end. He poked the rag doll with the hot stick and it caught on fire. The little girl burst out crying, dropped the doll and ran away in tears."

"Well, I though of how sad the dream was, but kind of forgot about it for awhile. But about two weeks later, a woman I know stopped by the house and gave me a dress she picked up at some yard sale or someplace. She said it was used, but might be nice for my two-year old to wear for play. I looked at the dress and got a funny feeling inside. The print material was just like what I remember from the dream. It was just like what the doll was wearing. I felt very strange just looking at it. I took it from my friend, held it up to look at it. I almost fainted. The front of the dress was exactly like the doll's. And, unbelievably, in the middle of the dress was a blackened spot and a small burn hole, as if someone had poked it with a hot stick!"

Completely baffled by the incident, Dottie was further convinced that there were supernatural events taking place in their home. She said she felt sorry for the ghost, feeling that it was a spirit at unrest. She wanted to see it find peace, and rest. But not in her home.!

The Stroheckers are Lutherans, but made a most interesting move in dealing with their spirits. They called upon a Monsignor at a Roman Catholic church in Reading. They asked if he would perform a house blessing, which the Stroheckers perceived as a mild form of exorcism, giving the ghost an idea that its presence was not desired. The priest obliged, and so did the ghost. After the blessing, the mysteries ended. No footsteps in the night. No disappearing scissors and tools. And no nocturnal visits from young spirits seeking playmates.

We contacted the Monsignor, and he confirmed that he did bless the home. He added that the procedure is simple and somewhat routine. He said that to his knowledge, there have never been any formal exorcisms performed by Catholic priests in Berks County.

And so, the Strohecker ghost story comes to an end. A happy and quiet end for the Stroheckers. But what about the spirit? Did it get the message and move along to haunt another home? Or is it finally, thanks to a simple religious procedure, on the other side and at rest? We will never know.

. . . or will we?

WITCHES' HILL

— Personal Research
May, 1982

From the crest of the hill which stretches between Windsor Castle and Virginville, the panoramic splendor of Berks County is at its finest. The light of a springtime sun illuminates forest and field below, casting shadows from the farmhouses and barns in the deep valley. But for the boxlike mobile homes that desecrate the bucolic vista, the view stretching 25 miles and beyond is of breathtaking, picture postcard quality.

This is the scene from atop this broad hill by day. When the sun retreats and the darkness tightens its quieting grip around the hill, it becomes a reviewing stand for the parade of nighttime splendor. The moon and stars dot the sky, meeting a horizon aglow with the distant auroras of the metropolitan areas of Allentown to the east and Reading to the south. Clusters of pinhead lights form villages and towns, and an occasional pair of tiny headlights can be discerned, as a car winds silently along country roads. But the silence — the almost morbid silence — is what one remembers best about this hill at night.

As the eyes need time to adjust from light to sudden darkness before night vision is attained, so must the ears be given time to become accustomed to the tranquillity of this spot after being held captive by the mechanical drone of the engine of the car which transported this ghost hunter to the hill.

So why go to this isolated spot far from any houses which could be called haunted? Why spend hundreds of words attempting to paint word pictures of a nondescript hill on just another quiet, dark spring night?

There is method to all of this. It all becomes relevent when we discover that it is May 1st, or in the German tradition, "Walpurgis Nacht." It is the night the witches come out to dance. And we are on the hill known for many, many years as "Witches Hill" in Windsor Township.

The vigil atop the hill ended just past midnight, and as the evening breeze washed over the hillside, the ancient superstition and more contemporary stories were retold while awaiting the witches' party.

The classic Walpurgis Nacht tales eminate from the Rhine River Valley and have been traced by folklorists back many centuries. After the region converted to Christianity, it is believed this pagan observance on May 1st was somehow retained. Walpurgis was noted on the hilltops by villagers and country folk who set bonfires and burned effigies of witches and other suspicious people in an effort to cleanse the region of the evildoers' activities.

Perhaps the early German settlers in this section of the county brought with them the knowledge and appreciation of the curious custom. As the generations between these original settlers and their

50

modern ancestors diluted many of these supersitions and practices, the traditions such as Walpurgis Nacht have been taken with less credulity and even scoffed at today.

But even today, the story of this hill remains a fascinating link between Berks County's past and present. Other links are all around the hill. Keen eyes can look down from atop the hill and spot "hex signs" on nearly every barn below. The "hex highway" of north Berks is a mile north of the ridge. And both the old and young of the area know this place as the hill where witches dance. The young are likely to call it simply "Witches Hill," while the older generation will cling to the dialectic "hexe Danz," or "witches dance hall." But monickers aside, its legend remains strong. And that legend consumes a wide range of supposition. Thrill-seeking teenage boys will tell vulnerable teen-age girls that they know of this hill near Windsor Castle where the car engine mysteriously stalls, conveniently near a shady grove just off the roadway. Or the old-timers claim that no vegetation grows at one spot atop the hill. Bobbing lights are reported seen atop the hill and even on the treetops of the hill. In 1954, historian Arthur Graeff wrote, "Years ago after a storm, the wheat stalks were flattened in spots. The old men would say 'Die Hexe hen dort gedanzt,' or, the witches danced there."

Perhaps the intrusion of the ghost hunter's party kept the witches from their revelry that particular May 1st. Whatever, there were no lights dancing on the treetops. No howling manifestations and no visible, audible witches. But there was time, and a perfect place, to recall yet another strange and somehow beautiful piece of Pennsylvania German — and Berks County — folklore.

THE GHOSTS AND LEGENDS
OF CHARMING FORGE

— Personal Interviews
June, 1982

It is difficult to maintain a twentieth century demeanor when walking through the spacious rooms and hallways of the Charming Forge mansion near Womelsdorf. There is an air of colonial majesty which thrusts the mind back hundreds of years to when this stately home served as the nucleus of the village which grew up along the Tulpehocken Creek. The life what was to become "Charming Forge" drew its breath from the "Eisenhammer" forge hammer built by Michael Miller and John Nikoll in 1749. This operation, powered by the waters of the Tully, was nurtured by Michael Rice and Garrett Brenner, who purchased the hammer from is founders. It later became the property of Michael Gross and Henry William Stiegel, who bought the forge in 1760.

Stiegel, renowned for his fine glassware which has carried his

52

name over two centuries, met an unfortunate financial fate after buying up thousands of acres and expanding the forge operation. He was pressured by his partners to right several economic wrongs and in desperation, Stiegel turned over his interest to a nephew named George Ege. Stiegel buckled under the debts owed to his partners and landed in debtor's prison in 1774. A year later, he was released by John Penn and eventually given a job by Ege, who had by that time purchased all interest in the forge and had enlarged it even more. It was Ege who built the stone mansion sometime between 1774 and 1777. In the quiet dell between the massive home and forge itself, a small village developed — a village not unlike the more notable Hopewell to the southeast — totally self-sufficient and comprised of several workers' cottages, a grist mill, boarding house, barns, an office, store, blacksmith shop and other buildings which pumped a very vibrant life into this remote area. Many of these buildings remain standing today, still providing the imagination with a glimpse of how life may have been in the century-and-a-half of village life at Charming Forge.

That village life passed as the forge became pitifully outmoded during the industrial revolution. Stiegel died in 1785, after about ten years as a humiliated former-owner relegated to being office manager employed by his nephew. Ege passed away in 1829. The forge continued to operate under Andrew Taylor, Simmon Seyfert and Richard Boone, executors of Ege's estate, until 1837. After that, Charming Forge fell into the hands of numerous owners, including George Keim, Henry P. Robeson, Clement Brooke and others. The forge passed into history in the 1880s.

In 1916 the property was purchased by Claude K. Taylor and John J. Sallade, and since then it has remained in the Sallade family, owned at this writing by Pearl Sallade Sensenig and Joan Sallade Everline. It now retains much of its colonial charm through the efforts of the family, which reclaimed the Georgian mansion and restored it to elegance.

But this is not a history book. It is a ghost book. So, where's the ghost?

It would be only a slight exxageration to say that a ghostly sensation grips the entire mansion, indeed the whole area. But it's difficult to deny that there is a sense of not just primitive industrial history here — but of corresponding human mystery that wraps Charming Forge in a feeling that makes it easy to visualize the prior life of this quiet place. It is said that Stiegel gave the name "Charming Forge" simply because of the land's charms. And those charms today not only saturate the landscape, but also those who take so much pride in its heritage.

The "big house" at Charming Forge is actually two buildings, joined into one in a way that only close examination can reveal any division. The oldest part of the house is the servants' quarters attached to the interior of the ironmaster's home by a corridor which extends perpendicular from the central entrance hallway. It was in this central corridor that we met Pearl and Joan. And, it is in the narrow, dark hallway to the servants' area where we shall meet one of the ghosts of Charming Forge.

The main hall is wide and ornate, with several large rooms leading from it. The passageway to the servants' quarters is entered from this main corridor through a giant arched door guarded by a frightening figure named "Sarah." Sarah stands silent, permanent sentry duty over this ghostly servants' hallway. Her body is of undetermined construction, her head is of papier mache, and she's dressed in fine colonial garb. She's a character who is a fixture at the mansion's fabled Halloween parties, and together with her companion named "George," who stands a similar vigil upstairs, is the concoction of the Sallade sisters, Pearl and Joan. It is no secret that beneath this frivolous paean to the supernatural, Pearl and Joan truly believe in the ghosts and legends of the property they have owned since 1960.

"Yes, we both believe in the ghosts," Joan says. "Pearl believes in a different way than I do." Joan, who is Pearl's junior by seventeen years, lives in the village's former office directly across the street from the mansion. It may be no surprise, then, when she says, "I think I believe more intimately about the ghosts here, and Pearl believes more ghost-storily." While Joan may have coined a word there, the fact remains that it is Joan who shares a more personal bond with the spirits in the mansion. Pearl, on the other hand, may romanticize a bit more about them. Pearl is a poet, and one of her works which we shall introduce later, is a lyrical approach to the ghost of Henry William Stiegel, which may be the most likely spirit to dwell in the shadowy rooms of the mansion. It is presumed that the glassmaker died on the property, and may even be buried there. But, there is a mysterious, unmarked grave in a Womelsdorf cemetery that may conceal his remains. More on that later.

"They very seldom come in here," said Pearl Sensenig as our ghost-hunting party entered the main parlor room on the mansion's first floor. She said that "they," or "it," the ghosts or ghost of the mansion, seem to have three favorite haunts. One very interesting such haunt is the corridor leading to the kitchen and the servants' quarters. According to a story handed down from a former servant who revisited the mansion in this century, there is good reason to believe the strange stories about this corridor. Again, Pearl Sensenig:

"A servant girl had been out here in the old kitchen at the fireplace and her skirt took fire. She ran through the hall and she died a few days later. And her spirit seems to be in here." Pearl adds that the incident was documented in forge records, as well as by the visiting ex-servant.

Well, the story is simple, but of the stuff that makes for a fine ghost story. But experiences of both Pearl and Joan add more supernatural spice to the plot.

"I came out of the kitchen one time," says Pearl, "and I was walking down the hallway and there was a black cloud above my head. I almost hit it. I went back in the kitchen and told some friends about it. It kind of scared me."

Pearl said it was a puff of black smoke, in no particular form, hovering over her head. She couldn't explain its origin, and was too frightened to determine what it may have been trying to do. Would it materialize into the form of a young girl? Was it a spectral remnant of the fiery death of the servant, trapped in time within the walls of the corridor? We shall never know.

Joan also tells a tale about this same hallway. "There's one time that I felt something. We were cleaning and I was in that hall and both doors were closed at each end. I was scrubbing the floor. All of a sudden I felt a scream welling up inside me. It wasn't as if I myself was screaming, but a scream just building up inside. I could feel it. It was very scary. Well, I was never in there alone again with the doors closed. I get a chill just thinking about it."

And so, the strange stories about this hallway remain indelibly etched in the sisters' minds. While it may be the power of suggestion at work, there really does seem to be something ghostly and ominous about this hallway. Our visit was made in springtime, after the winter cold had been purged by warmer air. Balmy breezes wafted through the spacious mansion that evening, but there was no doubt that this particular corridor was cooler and more damp than any other place in the house. But there again, the power of suggestion can be quite strong, right? Right?

The first floor of the mansion provided more stories.

"I was sitting in the kitchen in the main section of the house (not the kitchen in the servants' quarters) when I heard the screen door from the back yard open. I said, 'who's there?' I didn't hear anybody. So I went out to the main hallway and there was nobody there. But then I heard footsteps going up the stairs, so I started up after them. I got to the top of the third floor and I stopped. I looked in all the rooms there and on the second floor but there was nothing, nobody there."

Pearl's story leads us up the gently-rising staircase that spirals from the main entrance to the upper floors of the house. This staircase leads to the more elegant bedrooms and to more ghost stories. Pearl is not the only one to have heard footsteps on these stairs. One visitor to the mansion swears to have heard them. Even a skeptical Luther Sensenig (Pearl's husband) was once baffled by the mysterious creak and slam of the screen door which opens from the base of the stairs to the back yard. Two dogs which often accompany their masters on visits to the mansion are both affected by whatever or whoever is ascending the steps. One pooch once sat nervously at the bottom of the stairs, eyes riveted to a phantasmic focal point toward the first landing. There was nothing visible, but the dog's attention was centered for a long time to the unseen mark. Another pup simply refuses to have anything to do with the hallway and staircase, skulking away when brought there.

Let us now visit the second floor of the mansion, and listen to another tale from Pearl Sensenig as we enter what she calls "the most haunted room" of Charming Forge.

"When they built the ice house and smoke house out back, they disturbed Indian graves and the Indians put a curse on the place. And this is supposed to be a haunted room. They say in the days before electricity they couldn't keep a lamp lit in here."

It may be interesting to tie in another unexplained event with this story. Joan relates the story of what she laughingly calls the "blue glass ghost." It seems that a young girl, sensitive to the spirit world, was walking out of one of the rooms of the main house when in front of everyone's eyes a light bulb on a hallway fixture burst into thousands of pieces of blue glass. Simple electrical overload, or a modern application of the "couldn't keep a lamp lit" story?

Whatever, the strange stories are far from over. We walk farther down the main second floor hallway to another magnificent bedroom that will bring back a startling memory for a daughter of Pearl Sensenig's.

"This is where my daughter actually saw the ghost. She was sleeping there one night and she said she heard the bedroom door open. She opened her eyes and looked up and a man walked in the door, stood at the foot of the bed. He had a three-cornered hat on, and was dressed like in colonial days. He stood there, looked at her, then he turned away and walked toward the fireplace and disappeared." The plot really doesn't thicken much beyond that. It's all that really happened to one teenage girl in one room. But it would be enough to permanently scar one's memory of any pleasantness otherwise obtained inside the family-owned mansion.

The mansion becomes even more mysterious in a cosmetic way when the steps to the third floor are taken. It is believed that Stiegel himself occupied a small bedroom on this floor, and it can be speculated that his wandering spirit is the one that enters the mansion through the back door and hastily climbs the staircase to the third floor. Speculation indeed, but remember that Stiegel returned to Charming Forge a broken man; a former ironmaster there cast into poverty, imprisoned and given a job by his nephew who brought the forge, village and mansion into a glorious period. Remember too, that no one's really sure where Stiegel is interred. Therefore, it is conceivable that his ghost walks stealthily through the property, evading any contact with those who today care for the grandiose mansion he knew only in personal humility.

There are, in addition to the apparitional appurtenances of Charming Forge, some rather odd architectural quirks.

An old door in the servants' quarters has on it an "HL" hinge, a cleverly-worked wrought-iron piece designed in those two letters, fused together to form what Pearl says stands for "Holy Lord." She tells us these hinges can be found in many homes of this vintage, and were utilized to ward off evil spirits. Just a few feet away from this interior landmark is a section of broad floorboarding which has obviously been cut out, removed, and replaced. This was done a few years ago to see what was underneath the floor of this oldest section of the house. What was found were animal bones and general fill. But one woman present at the "dig" left the room hurriedly upon the discovery, and refuses to re-enter, maintaining that "something has been let out of the cellar!"

Charming Forge is awash with fascinating historical fact and fancy. There is a dingy, cramped attic that once was home for 34 Hessian prisoners of war, hired by the ironmaster from the government during the Revolution to build a millrace at the forge. Some of the German names around the area today are descended from these prisoners who eventually settled nereby.

And then, there is the legend of the "headless horseman" of Charming Forge!

It is generally acknowledged that this story probably falls deeply into the genre of "legend," but as any worthy legend does, it may actually have a basis in truth. Once again, we turn to Pearl Sensenig for the details:

"The housekeeper here had a nephew who came up from Virginia and worked in the office and fell in love with the daughter of the house. Of course, he had little money, so he said he'd go out west to make his fortune in the Gold Rush. He left, and they didn't hear from him for quite a while. But after a bit, his aunt got a letter that he was coming back. She told the girl that he was on his way. A few days later a horse came running through the village, foaming at the mouth. They finally caught him and retraced his steps and found the boy. The reins were wrapped around his neck, and he was dead from a broken neck. He had a lot of gold in his pockets."

Now, says Pearl, folks claim to still hear the frantic roar of a horse's hooves split a quiet night's silence. And they say there's a mysterious form riding on the horse's back — the form of the dead office boy frantically seeking the rendezvous with his loved one.

Pearl embellishes this story with a visit to another strange place, a few miles from Charming Forge. A visit to a cemetery in Womelsdorf where this "headless horseman" tale is post-scripted, and this entire chapter is enhanced by a non-ghostly, yet equally awe-inspiring account provided by the quiet, unassuming and ever-skeptical Luther Sensenig.

We now turn to Act Two, Set Two of our Charming Forge story, with the stage set on a windswept church cemetery in the borough of Womelsdorf.

For this writer, the visit to the graveyard is a geographical revelation. Womelsdorf, by route 422 standards, is a bypassed village of three-to-five minutes duration, embracing a slight rise on a nondescript plot of Berks County land. But from atop the cemetery hill, the rooftops and undulating skyline of the homes, shops, churches and small factories make Womelsdorf a compact country village reminiscent of European hamlets set amidst rolling hills and farmland. The vista erases all preconceived notions about this sleepy place and adds a new dimension to the town at Berks County's western gateway.

The Zion Lutheran cemetery is typical of any in this historic neck of Penn's Wood. Ancient tombstones with barely discernible inscriptions mingle with shiny granite monuments with crisply-cut names and dates of faceless peoples' births and deaths. As Pearl and Luther Sensenig lead the little investigative group across the green grass between the grave markers, Pearl reveals a most exotic talent that Luther possesses. He can detect the presence of a grave by using two wire clothes hangers, in much the same way as a "douser" using a divining rod finds water.

We'll soon see how Luther's unusual skill helps further develop this ghost story, but first a look at how his grave-finding is done.

He says he learned it from a gravestone maker in northwestern Berks, and claims no supernatural powers, just whatever gift it takes to make it actually happen. The two thin, metal hangers, not unlike any you'd have in your own closets, are bent at a 90-degree angle, in an L-shape. The short ends of each are inserted loosely into hollow wooden handles, and allowed to freely rotate within them. As Luther holds the hangers and handles very steadily, the hangers will point rigidly straight ahead over "normal" soil. But when a grave is located, the two hangers criss-cross together in the form of an X. After the few steps over a grave are taken, they straighten out once again. Another few steps, another grave, another criss-cross. And so on and so on. We watched attentively to detect any and all movement in Luther's hands, to see if any slight jerk or twist may result in the eerie motion of the hangers. But his fists were rock steady.

This technique helped in fostering a suspicion that Pearl has had for several years. In an "Ege" plot on the cemetery, there are five large monuments, all abreast in perpetual tribute to the name so attached to Charming Forge. All but one of the monuments are clearly marked with the names and birth/death dates of the deceased. Only a larger-than-life statue of a winged angel is devoid of any markings. The monument is equal in size to those beside it, but is oddly unmarked. This fact is perplexing to Pearl, a woman deeply involved in geneology. And Luther's skill adds even more confusion to the matter. Using that skill, he confirms that someone is buried at the foot of the winged angel. While there is no identification on the monument, there is a body buried beneath it.

When the ghost hunter suggests that Pearl believes the unknown grave may conceal the remains of Henry William Stiegel, she merely shrugs and moves along to the next mystery that binds the cemetery with Charming Forge's fables.

In the midst of a crop of brownstone grave markers is one with a timeworn carving of a riderless horse still visible on one side, while the name and dates are worn smooth on the other. Again, shrug is the silent answer to the question of whether this strange grave marker may memorialize the young man who never made it back to Charming Forge alive.

The shrugs are not to suggest that Pearl Sallade Sensenig, or her sister, Joan Sallade Everline, know more than they are willing to divulge. And the strange stories about the forge and its people should not, conversely, suggest that the women are telling more than they really know. It is merely legend, and one of Berks County's most interesting and lasting historical legends. Both women obviously cherish this legacy from a time that was at once more simple and more complex in many ways. Neither woman lives in the past, and the twentieth century has not overlooked Charming Forge — for better or worse. But the most fascinating element of Charming Forge's history just may be those stories of wayward spirits ensconced within and without the walls of the Charming Forge mansion. It is this possibility that these spirits exist that thrives in the souls of the women who keep this mansion still, er, charming, in every way.

Pearl's romantic attachment to the spirits that have come and may never have left the forge is obvious in the following poem penned by her several years ago:

'twas at the old Forge mansion
Standing proud upon a hill,
That the following experience
Set my beating heart athrill.

I was seated on the front porch
Gazing at the old pine tree,
When suddenly, a shadowy form
My vision seemed to see.

From the deepest, darkest spot
Of shadow neath the pine,
Came a lightly moving shadow
And a chill crept up my spine.

Heedless then of danger,
I rose on silent feet,
Tiptoed down the sidewalk
So the shadow I would meet.

And then I paused in wonder,
'twas a shade from out the past
'twas the ghostly, wraithlike Baron
Come to survey his holdings vast.

And I heard him softly murmur
As he passed me where I stood,
"An unmarked grave! A pauper!
I would show them if I could."

"I was once the rich, proud owner
of properties and mills.
I lived in style and grandeur
With furbelows and frills.

59

And the people paid me homage,
Yes, a great man — that was I."
Here he paused and meditated,
And I heard him deeply sigh.

Then his spoken thoughts continued
And I strained my ears to hear
This last message from a Baron
Who was a spirit for many a year.

"Alas," said he, "if someone
could only hear my plea,
I'd pray mankind be humble
and not try to live like me."

With one last burst of sighing,
He vanished into air.
And pondering his message,
I went back to my chair.

—Pearl Sallade Sensenig,
Womelsdorf, PA.

"DINE WITH THE SPIRITS"

Published Articles and
Personal Research
May, 1982

"Dine with the spirits."

That was once the motto of one of Berks County's most elegant and intriguing country restaurants. And, while "fine food and spirits" may be a hackneyed phrase used to sell the culinary charms of many a restaurant, the "spirits" of Brinton Lodge are of the apparitional, not the intoxicating variety. For according to popular legend, when one dines at a "cozy table for two" at Brinton Lodge, near Douglassville, several uninvited, invisible and innocuous guests, uh, ghosts, may join the party!

Since converted into a fine public dining establishment in 1976, the 18th century hotel/tavern has been acknowledged as a hostelry for more than one spirit. Indeed, regular visits by psychic researchers and mediums confirm that the place is, in the simplest of terms, a kind of rooming house for wraiths. It's said by those who can communicate with the spirit world that the hospitality Brinton Lodge has been, and is still known for proves quite inviting to those spirits who are "just passing through."

If any building ever "looked haunted," Brinton Lodge does. The huge structure's gables, peaks and windows are framed by massive trees that surround the building like twisted black fingers. Even by day,

60

there is an air of mystery about the land. The whirr of cars along route 724 has replaced the more romantic clip-clop of horse-and-buggy traffic that once brought patrons to the lodge in its earlier history. The swift-flowing Schuylkill just yards away guided the county's first Swedish settlers to the nerby Douglassville/Morlatton area. It is this same river that gave Brinton Lodge its darkest hour which may have unlocked the deepest secrets imprisoned within the building.

The ravaging flood of 1972 washed through the first floor of the 28-room building, and extensively damaged the elegant private club owned then by Caleb D. Brinton. The calamity so dampened Brinton's mortal spirit that he never re-opened the lodge. But Brinton's ethereal spirit supposedly still remains earthbound, and is today suspected of haunting the public restaurant. Some people connected with the lodge feel that Brintons ghost is merely protecting the place from the commonfolk who now flock to it for the sumptuous atmosphere and excellent cuisine provided by the heirs to the operation's reputation.

You see, Caleb D. Brinton ran a very exclusive lodge. He bought the building in 1927 from a well-heeled Philadelphia family which doubled the original size of the building and extensively remodeled it nine years before. He immediately established it as a "gentleman's club" and its clientele was hand-picked by Brinton himself. Well-known and influential types were whisked in and out of the lodge with their automobiles secreted in an adjacent barn. No one today can testify as to the calibre or identity or exactly who were the noted guests at Brinton Lodge, but the neighbors thereabouts did some wild speculating as to who went in and out, and what may have gone on inside this refuge for the rich and powerful.

This glorious past, clouded in mystery, was corroborated by a psychic who visited the lodge several years ago: "If these walls could only speak, they could reveal a truly fascinating history in part of which there has been great laughter and much music in the house at one time, and also there has been a period of much 'wheeling and dealing' amongst guests there, much of it stroking political favor and in those walls there have been arrangements made sometimes concerning matters of even national and possibly international importance."

With this legacy, Caleb Brinton's spirit may certainly be protective of the place. In fact, a brief spell of relative ignomony between the flood of 1972 and Brinton's death three years later may spark the spooking of the old innkeeper.

After Brinton's death in 1975, the property fell into the hands of a woman who had been Brinton's friend and confidante for many years. She was frail and occupied only the first floor of the building. During the short period of time she lived there, the legend of the lodge matured. No longer would neighbors ponder the internal activities of Brinton Lodge. Now, the building was scarred and humiliated by the flood damage and tenanted only by a reclusive woman who used but a corner of the sprawling estate. Passersby would swear they'd see ghostly shadows and strange movements in second and third floor windows. The lodge took on all the familiar trappings of a "haunted house."

An exhaustive renovating project began when new owners entered the picture in 1976. During the reconstruction, little evidence of anything supernatural surfaced. But as the restaurant neared completion, and the doors were to swing open for public use for the first time, the neighbors' suspicions were substantiated. A chef and a bartender, each spending nights there during the reconstruction, said they'd feel a strange chill sweep through the upper floor bedrooms. The downstairs lights would turn on and off with no human aid. They found an old-fashioned man's hat on the barroom fireplace mantel — when no one had been nearby to misplace it. Cigarette lighters flicked on to provide a guiding light in the pitch-dark attic would be extinguished by a sudden chilly breeze.

But it may be Caleb Brinton's determination to keep the "great unwashed" from his once-exclusive mansion that provides the basis for one of the most mysterious happenings in the early days of the public phase of Brinton Lodge's history. Just after opening week, a man and woman walked up to the lodge's main entrance at about 5:30 p.m. and expected to simply walk it. But no — the door was locked. They walked to a side door. It was locked. A back door. Locked. Frustrated, the man rapped on one of the doors. A puzzled waitress responded and explained that she had opened all the doors about an hour earlier! Could this have been Caleb's way of trying to keep "just anyone" out of his domain?

As flippant and circumstantial as these tidbits may be, there is far more breadth to the Brinton Lodge story. And, the building's ghostly guests and haunting history was vividly detailed by psychic researchers invited to the lodge by its owners.

Don Galloway, a psychic from Great Britain, was enlisted to assess the building's apparitional inhabitants. He did, and after a dramatic visit to the building in 1978, penned his observations in a letter to the proprietors.

Galloway prefaced his testimony with a bit of an introduction to his techniques: "Since all environments hold many emanations of the emotional level, memory wave-lengths and such of the people and situations which have passed through that atmosphere, I, as a medium, am hypersensitive to such vibrations."

The psychic was immediately greeted upon his arrival by an old friend. Standing in the lobby of the lodge, unseen by everyone but Don Galloway, was six-year old Carole, a little girl who often accompanies Galloway on his research expeditions. Carole died fourteen years ago. Carole is a ghost.

Further on, it wasn't long until the very subject of all the fuss was encountered.

"Walking alone along a corridor, I was pleasantly surprised to find myself suddenly accompanied by the presence of a quite heavily set gentlemen of medium-to-good height who walked with a slow, determined and somewhat authoratative step, was rather stiff in his back, and seemed to breathe rather heavily as if the end staircase up which he had seemed to come to join me would make him a little short in his breathing. I registered what sounded like the unusual name of Calum (unusual to me, an Englishman, anyway) but which later transpired to be Caleb."

"The man had an air of some self-satisfaction and also gave a strong feeling of approval of what had been done in recent times with the lodge and of the way in which life was now being conducted. He also seemed to me to be pleased indeed to have someone like myself present to whom he could convey his thoughts and feelings, as if liking the idea of sharing them.

"Nevertheless, I felt that he had been a man very sure of his own ideas and one who would never easily be swayed by others of perhaps more conventional style, and I think he could also have been somewhat close and secretive in his own earthlike dealing, but this did not make me feel his presence now was of anything but goodwill and contentment."

Throughout the building, Galloway felt the presence of those who had passed through the Brinton era of hospitality and who had also passed through this life onto the other side. Names like "Nichols, or Nicolson; Jacob or Jacobs; Theodore, Elizabeth and Gray." Army officers, aristocrats and others would flash in and out of the medium's mind. Various physical objects attached to the building's history would mentally materialize. Shards of two centuries were pieced together.

As benign as the spirit of "Caleb" may have seemed, the building's innermost riddles harbored less pleasant thoughts in the psyche of Don Galloway. There are many rumors and unanswered questions about the lodge. Was it really a station of the "Underground Railroad," providing a sanctuary for runaway slaves? Did a former gardener hang himself in the basement? Is a body buried in an unmarked grave somewhere on the property?

Galloway responded to these questions through further psychic processes. Yes, there probably was a body buried on the grounds. Yes, there was untold misery over the years. And yes, not all was agreeable in the halls of Brinton Lodge. As Don Galloway ventured onto the upper floors of the building, he discovered the other side of "the other side."

"There seemed to be nothing untoward here at first," Galloway observed upon ascending the staircase to the upper reaches of the lodge. "But the farther we proceeded along the landing, the cooler it became, and I developed a strong feeling of mental pressures or strain upon the head and then an icy coldness as we entered a small corner room. In here was a strong feeling of malevolence on the part of 'unseen forces' and I felt there had been a great deal of unhappiness there.

I also felt very much the presence of youthfulness there and realized this was from the spirit of a girl who had once lived there." The building's owner later confirmed to Galloway that a mentally disturbed young girl was kept in confinement in that room by her parents many years ago.

Galloway's attention was focused momentarily on a room marked "#200" on the second floor. He continued, "I also sense friction there between two other persons who had at one time lived in that part of the house. My only feeling was that this was from a man and a woman who had been in service here many years ago and who POSSIBLY would have been married.

"There has also been there a woman of great power and authority — almost like a madame at one time, and a gntleman who would have ruled with a rod of iron his underlings just as he himself was ruled by his wife or mistress. My impression was that at this period there would be black servants, or workers associated in the house also, these having also 'served' under a pretty tyrannical houseowner."

So, there is the good, the bad, the beautiful and the ugly in the annals of life at Brinton Lodge. Through the recent years, many researchers have come there, and evidence that the old building is inhabited by spirits continues to mount. One medium went so far as to surmise that the lodge is still functioning as it did earlier in its existence. While earthly beings wine and dine in the present, there are "wayward" ghosts paying their respects and seeking the conviviality they knew in the long-ago past, with Caleb D. Brinton still catering to a genteel clientele of an unseen world.

THE HAUNTED HAMPDEN FIRE STATION

— Newspaper Accounts and
Personal Research
March, 1982

The most common mental picture of a "haunted house" seems to be that of the vacant, old mansion on a windswept hill. More often than not, the typical ghost house is in the countryside, far from such urban amenities as streetlights, sidewalks and a profusion of people.

Ghosts, however, know no political boundaries. In the course of our ghost-hunting across the hills, mountains, valleys and back roads of Berks County, we tended to overlook the very heart of the county, the city of Reading.

The city's spirits hide in rowhomes, park lands and yes, even an abandoned firehouse. Most of them are elusive. Their stories are difficult to obtain, and often are simply too fragmented and embellished to assemble into any cohesive and conclusive narrative. There is a pesty poltergiest in a roomy Centre Avenue mansion. There's an old story told time and again by Central Catholic High School students of the ghost that walks the halls, rooms and garden of that Hill Road school. On Clover Alley, between Moss and Tenth Streets, there is the story of a turn-of-the-century murder of a woman that has produced reports of "wails and groans" from the afflicted house.

But the most facinating ghost story to come out of the city of Reading in recent years is that of the ghost of Edward C. Dell at the Hampden Fire Company building at 11th and Greenwich Streets.

The Hampdens' building dates back to 1887 and is on the National Register of Historic Buildings. The character of the Hampden Fire Company as a cog in the city's volunteer fire fighting operation has been sullied recently by the closing of the building and the consolidation of companies. The fate of the building itself remains in the balance, while the structure agonizes from neglect and apathy. The building violates the same safety and fire codes established by the fire officials who once worked and slept inside it. But the history and pride of the men who served in the Hampden ranks remains unshakeable, as the yellowed photographs, tarnished trophies and dusty mementoes inside the meeting room of the building so graphically illustrate.

Whatever may happen to the fire station, it is likely that the spirit of Edward Dell, which allegedly inhabits the spacious building, will remain on guard eternally. It is here that Dell spent the best years of his life on earth, and it was in the service of his beloved fire company that he gave his life.

Dell's career in the Reading Fire Department is legendary. Born in 1895, he moved into the city at age 14 and got a job as a pretzel baker at Bachman's. In 1915, he joined the Hampden Fire Company as a volunteer, and was hired as a driver two years later. Dell served 14 years as a driver, 7 as an assistant Foreman, 8 as a chief engineer and was elected second deputy fire chief in 1931. When not living at his sister's Green Street home, the tobacco-chewing, motorcycle-riding, railroad buff would be on station at the "Hamdies." Even on his days off, he'd respond to fire calls. Dell was equally popular with the ladies and the kids of the neighborhood. The affable World War I veteran would be first on the streets on a hot day, with wrench in hand to open fire hydrants and let the cooling waters flow for curbside fun for the youngsters. Dell was respected by those in the fire department who worked with him. It's said that he never drank, smoked or swore. He admitted once that he wasn't very religious, but, in words attributed to him, "I'm a Catholic at heart."

That kind and good heart of Edward Dell's ceased to beat on December 2, 1953, the sixth anniversary of his election to the post of Fire Chief. Dell and partner Nathaniel Rhoads had finished dinner at the Rhoads home when the call came: A smoke condition on East Wyomissing Boulevard. With the chief at the wheel of his car, Dell and Rhoads sped to the scene. But something went wrong along the way. As they rounded what was then a traffic circle at Fifth and Penn Streets, Dell was stricken. In vain, he jammed the gears into neutral and slammed on the brakes. The car smashed in the front of a bus.

Emergency crews arrived and Dell was rushed to the Reading Hospital where it was determined he died of a cerebral hemorrhage.

Dell's funeral procession to the Tenth and South Cemetery was one of the largest in the city's history. Friends and relatives, fellow firefighters, and those whose lives were in any way touched by Edward Dell came to pay last respects. Perhaps as a prelude to the ghostly legend that was to evolve later, Dell's burial did not proceed without incident. It's recorded that as they tried to close Dell's casket, there was a hitch. The ceremonial fireman's helmet placed on Dell's chest prevented the easy closing of the coffin, and after some rearranging, the job was done and Reading Fire Chief Edward C. Dell was laid to rest in Peace.

Or was he?

There are those today who feel that Dell's spirit is still very much alive and it's based primarily on an old firehouse yarn that maintains that since the chief never completed that "last run," his spirit still wanders on this side of eternity, seeking the final serenity.

However decrepit and forlorn the Hampden Fire Company's once-majestic headquarters may be, and whatever fate holds in store for it, the building is in itself a monument to Edward Dell. Outside, floating in a sea of chipped paint, is a bronze plaque with Dell's likeness and a tribute to "39 YEARS OF FAITHFUL SERVICE TO THE READING VOL. FIRE DEPT." Inside, a large photo portrait of the late chief dominates an architecturally stunning second-floor meeting and game room. Throughout the building, there is the sense of uncertainty and mystery that gives the hint of something supernatural.

Many of the sounds that catch the uninitiated offguard when spending an otherwise quiet night at the vacant building can be rationalized away. The bumpety-bumpety-bump is a shaky window frame. The shoosh is air — one of a dozen drafts from a dozen sources. The electrical appliances and heating system provide more strange noises. But more identifiable sounds that could be more attributed to ghostly events have had a handful of firefighters who have worked and slept there during its waning years perplexed. As the legend of Edward Dell was passed on to this newer generation of firefighters from the last, the younger men came to blame more and more of the strange happenings at Hampden on the playful ghost.

Most firefighters are creatures of routine. The discipline of their jobs demands that. Edward Dell was of that mold. He would spend his idle hours at the fire station in a wooden chair in the dayroom, propped up precariously against he wall, the chair tottering on two legs. One firefighter who is a believer in the ghost of Dell, said he'd do the same thing. In the same chair. Against the same wall. All of a sudden, while not particularly off-balance, the chair would slide from beneath him, flipping the fireman to the floor. There have been times that the nightly routine of closing a second-floor bathroom door was broken up by the door being open in the morning. Nobody had used the facilities during the night. There are what firefighters have called "definite human footsteps" climbing the steep wooden stairs with nobody in sight. The crash of billiard balls on an unattended, empty upstairs table has shattered the silence of several nights.

In that same room is the portrait of Edward Dell. On a recent winter's night, that portrait wobbled and fell to the floor near some firefighters who watched in frightened amazement. The night of this incident was December 2 — the anniversary of Dell's death.

There is no doubt that the Hampden building is big, drafty and hard to heat, but besides costing the city a lot of money for fuel, the heating quirks of the place add another element to the supposition that the building is haunted. At no time, say those who have tended to the building in recent years, have they been able to get the inside temperature higher than 68 degrees. Even when the thermostat was turned up to 98 degrees, the best the room temperature could do was 68.

Doors on the inside and outside of the bulding have either opened mysteriously, or have just as strangely, refused to open with ease. Even the huge garage door of the fire station has been known to open on its own — a phenomenon attributed to a C.B. radio signal or some other electrical device.

Still, there are enough unexplained and unrationalized occurrences from the annals of the building that keep the legend of Dell's ghost very strong. Some firefighters who served as transients at the building, unfamiliar with its many idiosyncracies and yet aware of the ghostly stories about it, have simply rfused to sleep inside the "haunted Hamdies." They'd find all-night "busy work" inside, whistling loudly while they evaded sleep and possibly a spooky encounter. They'd sit on the outside bench through the night, doing anything to avoid shutting their eyes inside the place. Unbeknownst to them, however, was the fact that the only man who ever actually died at the fire station, died on that very sidewalk bench!

Another veteran fire driver, now deceased, told his colleagues of the time he actually saw the ghost of Dell. He was asleep in the bedroom of the station when he was rudely awakened by a violent shaking of his bed. He looked up and saw Dell, dressed in white, warning of a fire call about to come in. The fire driver rubbed his eyes incredulously, and was within minutes back asleep. But his sleep was again interrupted by . . . a fire call!

One of the true believers in the Dell ghost once told a newspaper reporter, "I don't fear ghosts, if, indeed, they do exist. I am of the opinion that Edward isn't going to hurt anyone, and least of all another firefighter. He was a good chief from the old school who did his duty. He just never completed that final run!"

DER SCHPUK VON LANGESCHAMM

— Arthur Graeff Story

The German language has given us one of the most familiar and ominous words of our ghostly glossary: poltergeist. By definition, the word means "uproarious spirit." A poltergeist is merely a noisy ghost. Somehow, and some believe via a Holland Dutch word, we came to dub some spirits as "spooks." This word was then adapted by the Pennsylvania Germans as "schpuk."

This little linguistics lesson is nothing more than a preface to this legend of "Der Schpuk von Langeschamm," or, the ghost of Long-swamp.

Longswamp Township is your basic, average sleepy rural township, ripe for the supernatural picking. It is typical of those areas that even under the light of the sun seen to be enveloped in quiet repose. Wandering through Longswamp, it is easy to harken back to an earlier age and conjure up the kind of story that has endured through the centuries to this day.

The ghost of Longswamp surfaced in a fine poem by John Birmelin. Written in the Pennsylvania "Dutch" dialect, the poem vividly described the story of an evil man who was believed to be a foreman or master at the Mary Ann Furnace. This man is alleged to have pushed a furnace worker into a boiling cauldron at the furnace as a fatal punishment for a simple misdeed. He is described as a hateful employer who, even after death, continued to pursue his reign of terror.

For the story, we turn to the writings of Dr. Arthur Graeff:

Only the pen of a Birmelin and only your dialect can record the eerie things that happened in the Longswamp. We shall not attempt, here, to translate the ghostly and ghastly doings of the bony spectre who demanded to be appeased by the living. He would rest only if supplied with three objects: A broom, a pair of shoes and a straw hat.

After many peccadillos the spook was finally captured in the granary of a barn at Henningsville, Berks, and a "priest from the mountain" was summoned to lay the evil one to rest.

Four strong men carried the skeleton form to the top of Der Diehle Kopp, or Diehl's Head Mountain, which rises like a wall above the Longswamp. There, with incantations, the priest drew a "banning circle," or a charmed circle around the prostrate form and, after the flurry of some leaves an open space was cleared at the peak of the mountain.

There, with mysterious words and gestures, the priest dispatched the apparition forever and he was destined to shovel coal in the nether regions for all time to come.

Even in this era, reports of strange sightings on and around Diehl's Mountain filter through the reality of the day. Others have reported a ghost walking through the family cemetery in which the furnace foreman is interred.

THE HILL ROAD HAUNTING

— *Personal Research*
July, 1982

Most people don't keep count on the number of automobile accidens that occur in front of their house. Most people don't think much when they misplace a set of keys. Just plain forgetfulness or creeping feeblemindedness, they say.

But for a family residing in a home just over the Reading city limits, these seemingly minor events and much more accounted for over a year of uneasiness and in some cases, near panic.

The Hill Road section of East Reading was hard hit by vacancies during the Great Depression. As owner after owner abandoned the large homes that dotted the eastern slope of Mount Penn, more and more "haunted house" stories entered the imaginations of youngsters living in the austere rowhomes in the city below. It was pre-TV, and the tales of these roomy, empty, ofter boarded-up derelict dwellings provided vivid entertainment. The more daring neighborhood "toughs" would even hike the hill and venture inside some of these scary buildings to prove their fearlessness. But the more time these youngsters put between the Depression and their own futures, the more these stories became mere memories. The more that prosperity saw the rebirth of Hill Road, the less was heard of haunted houses.

Don't try to tell Sherry and Richard about this haunted heritage of Hill Road. They're relative newcomers to the area, occupying their stately half-century old home for a little more than four years. For the intelligent young executive and his wife, however, the neighborhood welcoming party was anything but cordial.

Specifically, the chain of events that the couple speaks of began to unfold when their daughter was brought into the home after her birth at a city hospital. That night, there was an auto accident on the corner in front of their home. "Hmmm," said a neighbor, "there's only been one or two other accidents up here in the thirty years I've lived here!" Well, more and more accidents took place at that corner. In the first fourteen months Richard and Sherry lived there, fourteen accidents — three on just one night!

Of course, the couple didn't attach any supernatural explanation to this. It was happenstance. More traffic. Whatever.

There was no reason to feel that any spook was responsible for another incident which took place after the new owners had remodeled the home and, with the new baby, had begun to settle in. A wristwatch, lost by Richard several months before, suddenly turned up in a logical spot and was found by Sherry and placed on a shelf near the front door. Sherry was anxious to tell Rich about her discovery when he arrived home from work, but when he walked through the front door and was greeted by a wife with some good news, both were treated to a baffling event. The watch was, again, nowhere to be found.

It had disappeared from the shelf where Sherry was sure she had placed it. No one except the baby was in the house that day she found it, and Sherry swears she didn't inadvertently move it. Upon hearing the story, Rich was confused. Sherry began to wonder.

Similar incidents came in rapid order. One night, Sherry went to bed and, as on any other night, she took off her glasses and placed them on the dresser. She woke up in the middle of the night, touched her face and discovered that she was wearing her glasses. Now Sherry was confused. She took off the glasses, placed them on the dresser. Again she went to sleep. Again she awoke to find her glasses on her face. She repeated the entire process again, and woke up one more time — with her glasses on.

Oh yes, back a couple of paragraphs: Remember the wristwatch lost, then found, and then lost again? About three months after the incident, the watch ws found again, lying in the middle of a bed in a room rarely used by the family.

The story does not end here — not by any stretch of the imagination. And stretch the imagination is what was necessary for Sherry and Rich to do for them to fathom the next series of events.

"One night, around one o'clock in the morning, the dog woke up," Sherry remembers. "You know how sometime they'll just growl like they hear something? A kind of quiet 'grrr?' Well, he woke us up, and he jumped off the bed and he was pacing back and forth in the hall upstairs. We could hear somebody — it sounded like an old woman — moaning and crying. We both heard it."

"I said to Rich, 'what is that?' It definitely wasn't a child . . . it wasn't our child. One minute it sounded like it was inside the house, the next like it was outside. The poodle went from a soft growl to a real nasty growl up and down the hallway."

Suddenly, Sherry and Rich were wrapped in an icy grip. The room turned freezing cold. "It wasn't like an ordinary cold, you know, it was like you were cold from the inside out. It was a feeling I've never felt before or since. It was like my bones were cold. I just couldn't warm up," Richard says.

Still the dog growled. Still the faint moaning, crying sound. Still the icy chill. Eventually, the warmth of a summer's evening returned, the moaning ceased and the dog nervously retired for the night.

Looking back on the moments which surely seemed like months to the two, Sherry remembers the eerie sound: "It was the sound of an old woman crying and mumbling. You really couldn't understand it. But that's definitely what it was. It was very frightening. Through it all, we were riveted to the bed, waiting for it to be over. I think we were too frightened to even turn a light on."

The incident piqued the couple's curiosity. Had anyone — an old lady, perchance — ever died in the home? Could there be a reasonable explanation for such a ghostly incident?

The answer to this question came from a neighbor who told them yes, an old woman had lived there in recent years and although she didn't die inside the home, she did eventually succumb to injuries sustained in a fall down the stairs which lead to what was her second-floor bedroom.

Rich feels the strange happenings inside the home began when their newborn child was brought home. Both Rich and Sherry toy with the idea that the spirit of the former resident may have been disturbed by the intrusion of the infant.

The events that followed may have added credence to that hypothesis.

The baby had been placed in her crib and Rich wound up the music box of the mobile that bobbed and swayed over the baby's head. The tinkling notes and near hypnotic effect of the mobile lulled the little girl to sleep.

At some point well into a sound sleep, Rich was gently awakened by a familiar sound. It was the music from the mobile. Wafting through the night's silence, the music box that had wound down hours before, began to play. Perplexed, Rich rose to see what could be seen. But he knew there was no way the toy could "rewind" on its own. He had heard it grind to a slow silence before he fell asleep, and there was no way the baby could wind it.

Rich approached the door of the nursery. As he turned the knob and swung the door open, the music stopped. He was taken back by that, as might be understood. So, too, was he miffed by the fact that the closet door in the child's room was wide open. He and Sherry had made a point of closing this closet door when they tucked the baby in.

Rich wondered out loud what was going on. He checked to make sure the baby was safe, and looked at the music box. It was totally wound down with no chance of squeezing another note out of it by winding it tightly in the wrong direction.

Perhaps, he thought, he dreamed of the music. Perhaps the compression of opening the room door opened the closet door. He quietly closed the closet door until it clicked shut, placed a kiss on his index finger and touched it upon his daughter's forehead and retreated to his and Sherry's room.

Rich had just begun to doze off again when once more the sound of the music box drifted into his room. A harried father repeated the entire episode just related and grew more frustrated and frightened. Again the music stopped when he opened the door, the closet door was open, and the baby slept through it all.

Incredibly, an hour or so after Rich went to bed for the second time, the strange sequence was repeated once again. By this time, Sherry had become aware of the night's strange events. There was no sense of raw fear, as Rich explains, "Other things had happened up to this point, and we more or less accepted the fact that somebody else was living in that house besides us!"

But who could it be? The couple generally accepted their own, convenient, "little old lady" spirit as that which walked the halls, engaged in nocturnal pranks and groans, and made life — shall I say — interesting for them.

Another answer, or at least what appeared to be an educated guess, so to speak, came from a nationally-known and respected psychic who may be recongized best by his stage name, "The Astonishing Neal."

The scene was Richard's company Christmas party. The players were Rich and Sherry, a group of their friends, and Neal. The couple had shared some of their ghostly stories with these close friends, but no one at their table had any previous contact with Neal. As the performer/psychic sought a volunteer/victim from the audience, the friends egged Sherry onstage. While in the act, Sherry and Neal engaged in routine mind-reading, mysticism and showy tricks. The act continued, but lurking in Sherry's mind was the question she was afraid to ask this man with these unique senses and power. It may be he who could shed light on the unanswered questions about who, if anyone, shared their home with them.

Neal's act ended, as did Sherry's hopes that she could gather enough nerve to ask about the goings-on in her house. But again the group of friends urged her to pose the question. After the show, she approached Neal. In order not to reveal too much in the question itself, the query was carefully worded: "Neal, can you tell us something about, uh, some of our, uh, surroundings?"

Afraid that the question was too vague, Sherry was uneasy as Neal stared into her eyes for a painfully long period that in reality was a few seconds.

"Oh, you mean the haunted house you live in?" Neal's voice broke the awkward quiet.

Neal looked at Sherry and Rich, "Wait a moment, I'll tell you something about it." The psychic squinted slightly and seemed to stare into another dimension — another time and place.

"I am going back . . . back to a war . . . the Revolutionary War . . . I see a soldier . . . I see many soldiers . . . I see a prison . . . more soldiers . . a musket . . . cabins . . . foreign soldiers . . ."

Neal's thoughts and visions trailed off as a hollow sensation built up inside both Sherry and Rich. Neal cocked his head and smiled as the couple looked at each other in a way they had never before. Their emotions confirmed to both of them that the psychic may have satisfied their search for an answer to their mystery. They gathered their senses, quietly thanked Neal for his time, clasped hands reassuredly and walked away, never revealing to Neal one very salient fact of this fantastic tale. It is a fact that I have not yet revealed to you, the reader, either. It is the fact that Sherry and Rich live in a home on land once occupied by hundreds of German mercenaries taken prisoner during the Revolution. Their home is in a section of town called Hessian Camp!

"LIZZIE — "

THE POLTERGEIST OF LINCOLN ROAD

— Personal Research
July 1, 1982

The house was built in the middle of the nineteenth century, and was the summer home of a prominent Philadelphia attorney whose permanent residence in New Jersey is a registered state landmark. During the era of its existence as a summer retreat, its only year-round occupant was a tenant housekeeper. During its current era as a stately residence along Lincoln Road, Exeter Township, its residents include those of both the property owner and a ghostly cohabitant who has, at various time, been heard, felt and seen!

The last of the family line that built and lived in the home for more than a century left several years ago. The old man died and his widow retreated to retirement in the sunbelt. The man was considered some-what of an eccentric by his neighbors, and there seemed to be a sense of mystery about what went on behind the white fence that surrounds the place. But the neighbors sensed only the tip of the ethereal iceberg that consumed the wits of the man who last owned the property and who was bedeviled for several months by a poltergeist he affection-ately dubbed "Lizzie."

"I gave whoever or whatever the name of Lizzie because I found out somehow that the last owner's first wife was named Elizabeth. Supposedly, she got sick and the nurse who came to take care of her eventually beccame the man's second wife. Well, I just came to the conclusion that all the carrying on was Elizabeth, because she was unhappy and never really left."

The story is told by Bob Boyer, a tall, refined man who purchased the home and made many cosmetic and structural changes to accom-modate his twentieth-century lifestyle. There was no modern kitchen in the place, so that was one of the first considerations of remodeling. It was also one of the first chances Lizzie had to torment the new occupant.

"She'd come down the back stairway in the house, where the old cookstove-and-pantry kitchen was — which was now my dining room. One time, my friend said he came down the steps early in the morning and stopped. There was a woman standing at the cookstove. She was just kind of moving pots and things around on the stove. She turned and looked at my friend and he looked at her and — poof — she was gone!

"Another time, she was taking dishes out of a cabinet, which once had doors, but had been converted into an open hutch. But my friend said that when he saw her there, the cabinet doors were on it and she was opening the doors and putting dishes on the table. He said when she glanced over at him, she just smiled and vanished. So did the. cabinet doors."

73

Bob said he never actually saw this ghost he calls Lizzie. The incidents he recalls are more of a poltergeistic nature, but others who lived in the home for however brief a period from time to time have indeed seen apparitions, as witnessed in the previous paragraphs and more to come.

While he never actually saw Lizzie, Bob would certainly feel her presence:

- He'd be playing the electric organ and suddenly the power would shut off — the cord jerked from the wall socket by an unseen force.
- He'd be reading a book on a quiet night and the lamp's plug would be pulled from its socket.
- The water heater would mysteriously switch itself off.
- The swimming pool filter would shut down.
- Outdoor spotlights would switch themselves on and off.
- He'd misplace a book and several months later find it stuffed deeply between the box spring and mattress of his bed. He knew he didn't put it there.
- He'd misplace his car keys and find them weeks later in the freezer section of his refrigerator.

Believing that some of the occurrences may have been the result of electrical malfunctioning, electricians were called in to check the system. They reported that everything from the pole to the fusebox to the interior wiring was in fine shape.

"Other time, I'd be playing the organ and — you know when somebody walks up behind you and just stands there and you can just feel it? Well, I felt that many times while seated at the organ. I had two Dobermans and they'd just go berserk. These things were annoying — nothing frightening, nothing had ever happened — but I would just talk to her. You know, I'd say 'Okay, Lizzie, knock it off. Leave me alone!'"

When company came to call, Lizzie would be at her most demonstrative best.

"Apparently she didn't like changes. When I had company, she'd turn the lights on and off, and it would get a lot more serious than that. Some friends from Morgantown stayed in the house one-half of one night and NEVER came back again — daytime, nighttime, no time!

"The people came to stay overnight, but in the middle of the night they came out of the room screaming, yelling, carryng on. They told me the big four-poster bed was jumping up and down off the floor. This happened three times. Well, they left and never came back. The same thing happened to me later on. The bed raised up — honest to God — but it wasn't shaking, it wasn't wiggling. It actually raised up off the floor a few feet and dropped and started pounding — boom ... boom ... boom!"

As Bob tells the story today, his speech is charged with emotion. It seems obvious that something had happened that shook his nerves at their very roots.

After a while, the unearthly incidents in the house became fairly routine. For its owner, the house and its cantankerous occupant could provide few real surprises. But for the many visitors who came in and out of the bachelor owner's life, there would be many, many surprises.

"My sister is very religious and doesn't believe in any of this ghost stuff," Bob says. "She said it was the work of the Devil. She and her husband and two kids came to stay one night. She was downstairs alone, her husband and kids were asleep upstairs. I was working the midnight shift that night. She swears she heard footsteps on the hallway over her head. She checked, and everyone was in bed. She called me at work and I told her to calm down, it was just Lizzie. She was scared. She said the house had demons inside. Who knows what she really things?"

The disembodied footsteps were nothing unusual to Bob, and several others heard them in the second floor hallway and on the staircases on several occasions.

"On the third floor there was a door to the attic with a big, old, heavy latch. Quite often, you'd hear the latch close — it would echo throughout the house. Then you'd hear footsteps walk right down the stairs. Then they'd turn and go down the hallway. You'd hear them clear as, well, footsteps!"

There was one room in the house that Bob completely avoided. "It was an evil room," he says. It's the only room in the house that he did not remodel. "When I'd go into that room, I'd get a strange feeling. I wouldn't go in there to clean, to paint, nothing!"

"At night, some nights, you'd hear a kind of a whining. It would start out low and it would just kind of grow in intensity and get louder. At first, it was a woman crying, and then there was arguing and then she'd start screaming and then you'd hear a man's voice. It was kind of muffled. You couldn't quite make out what they were yelling about, but it was distinct enough that it was a back-and-forth confrontation between a man and a woman."

While Bob stayed out of that room, a friend would regularly stay in the room while visiting. The friend also regularly complained of strange nightmares, but could never remember any details. Bob recalls, "Many, many times he'd wake up screaming and running out of the room. I tell you, it was an evil room."

Actually, Bob was not the first owner after the family line that had lived there for nearly one hundred years. A previous owner, who bought the home and spacious grounds in hopes of settling in, left hurriedly, selling to Bob at a sacrificial price. She told him she actually saw the ghostly figure of a man, clad in a white suit and white hat and brandishing a shotgun, materialize from the woods behind the house. "She was spooked out of the place," Bob says.

This backyard apparition reminded Bob of another episode that sent chills through the body of a female visitor one day.

"There was a pool in the backyard, and this girl friend of mine was floating on a raft. All of a sudden she came running into the house and was hysterical. We asked what was the matter. She said, 'Nothing . . . but I think I'd better go home.' Well, finally she told me. She was out in the pool and she happened to look up to a third floor window and she saw a figure pull the curtain back and stand to the side of the window, looking at her. I said she was crazy — nobody was up there and there aren't even curtains up there! She said she went over to the deck of the pool and put her glasses on. She said she saw the figure go across the window to the other side. I told her to calm down and we'd go upstairs and I'd prove there was nobody and no curtains up there. We went up — she was shaking like a leaf — but there was nothing. No curtains, nothing. The room was completely empty."

For various reasons, Bob decided to move from the spooky house. He recalls, "When I put the house up for sale, I think Lizzie got really upset, because she really started acting up.

"I looked out the front window one morning and thought a car had struck the white board fence in front. I got dressed and went outside. The fence was completely dismantled. Boards were neatly stacked. It was as if some big wind or percussion just pushed the fence neatly together. I was angry, but I rebuilt the fence."

Bob says Lizzie may still be up to her tricks. After he sold the house, about a week after the new owners moved in, he received a phone call. The whole front fence was blown out. There was no actual damage, it was just as if some unearthly force jolted the fence back and neatly dismantled it on the front lawn. He remembers the words from the new owners that just made him chuckle a bit, "You know, Bob, this place is kind of strange!"

So, you be the judge. Was the activity in and around this Lincoln Road home just a product of Bob's imagination? Were his friends' imaginations likewise sparked by Bob's stories? Or does a spirit still walk the halls and staircases and haunt the rooms of this century-old house? As in any other ghost story, you either believe . . . or you don't.

A FATHER, A SON,
AND AN OLEY GHOST

— Collected Stories
August, 1982

Along a lonely country road then known as "Long Lane," which connected the village of Oley to the Oley Turnpike, walks the ghost of a young woman doomed to an eternal search for the boy she loves. This spirit, they say, can drive a person to death, if one dares to touch her.

The story was passed along many years ago by Ethel Guldin, of Reading. She tells of a young man in love with the hapless young woman during the American Revolution. They were neighbors, child-hood sweethearts, and intended to marry in the springtime that would follow a long winter of war. But, so impressed with the colonials' struggle was the young man that he enlisted in General Washington's army — against the pleas of his fiancee. Seeing his duty and responsibility, he remained firm on his intentions and prepared to depart for the service of his country.

He was due to meet Washington's troops along the Oley Turnpike, and his heartsick lover walked with him on Long Lane, where they bade farewell to each other with a kiss. They promised to meet at the same place the following May, when they would reunite and wed.

The kiss on Long Lane proved to be their last. The young lady waited through the winter and when May arrivd, began her daily vigilant stroll along the road from which he departed, awaiting the joyous return. The vigil went far past the warming days of May and into the hot days of summer. It was July when she was told that her intended husband was shot and killed in battle. Shattered, the young woman felt no reason to continue living, and it is said she simply wasted away and died, broken hearted.

But her confused spirit remained earthbound, according to Oley Valley folklore. One night, a man was walking down Long Lane, near the spot the two lovers kissed for the final time, and met a young woman dressed in what was described as a white wedding (or burial) gown. It was obvious that she was quite sad, and offered only a pitiful smile and her limp hand. The man reached out, touched her with a pathetic handshake, and quickly went home to tell his story. Within days, the gent who met and touched this spirit of Long Lane was dead, the victim of a freak accident.

This same ghost still haunts Long Lane, and on any given night between May and July, she can be seen maintaining a hopeless and endless watch for her fallen beau. If you are fortunate enough to see her, by all means offer your sympathy and look — but be sure not to touch!

IN THE STORIED Oley Valley is what might be called a legendary tree. And if it is at all possible for a tree to be "haunted," the Sacred Oak must certainly be. It is, at least, haunted by the history and ceremony it has witnessed in its extraordinary life span, and if it could speak it would tell tales that would fill several volumes of folklore and legend.

Located in a meadow to the rear of a farmyard near Oley, the solid tree stands out in its environs. Its trunk measures more than twenty feet in circumference and its branches spread out to a distance of one-hundred feet. Two small monuments mark its heritage. The owners of the property along the Friedensburg Road upon which the oak stands say that each year several individuals and even groups of historical and nature buffs visit the Sacred Oak to marvel at its size, endurance and legendry.

The Sacred Oak, well over two-hundred years old, is probably the oldest living landmark in the Oley Valley.

The Indians communicated with their almighty spirit via the limbs and roots of the giant Chestnut Oak. At the base of this tree, the red men came with their ailments while medicine men performed their traditional rites. Warring or feuding tribes smoked the peace pipe at the Sacred Oak, seeking guidance from the great spirit. Many a squaw's life was spared from disease beneath the sheltering branches of the Sacred Oak. Treaties were signed there, and it was the focal point of the Oley Valley Indian folk tales.

This valley, one of America's most fertile areas, may also be one of its "spookiest." Many Berks Countians will recall childhood tales of the supernatural eminating from the hills and dales surrounding the village of Oley. The most incredible story, however, involves one of the earliest families to settle in the area.

THE TALE IS TOLD by a contemporary folklorist from Oley, and with apologies to those who draw a firm, hard line between fact and folklore, here is the legend of the Keim legacy, as told to this writer.

Johannes Keim was one of the first residents of what is now the Oley Valley, coming to this soil shortly after William Penn received his land grant for his now-famous "wood."

Johannes' descendant, John Keim, heir to a marvelous estate, lived with six daughters throughout the last part of the last century. Their home, located near Lobachsville, still stands in all its ancient splendor.

After John Keim's death, somewhere near the turn of the century, his daughter, Betsy, maintained the homestead. She was, according to one Oleyite, "a massive woman, maybe three-hundred pounds, with a beard down to here . . ." After he motioned to a spot two buttons from his collar, I thought that she might have been, in fact, the only "supernatural" being in the Keim legend. I was wrong. Dead wrong, as they say!

The Keim family was rich. So rich that before his death John Keim hid over $100,000 in silver at various places throughout the home. The Keim estate also included several acres of valuable hardwood, which no Keim could ever sell for lumber. John Keim so loved this stand of trees that he stipulated it in his will.

After the last surviving family member died, the estate was sold at auction. Oddly enough, a lumber dealer bought the rights to the precious woodland. He proceeded to level the timber for sale to a German furniture concern. The Keim legacy was violated, and John Keim was not about to take it lying down.

One gloomy night, according to witnesses, John Keim arose from his grave, eerily displaying his abomination with the act. Apparently, the cries of "ti-i-imber" had awakened Keim from his peaceful rest.

His spirit could be, and supposedly still can be seen on selected evenings. Three months after he died, neighbors reported passing the house and seeing John's face in the window, nonchalantly shaving in

78

the moonlight. Yet another farmer, who was tilling the soil of the auctioned farm, months after it had received new owners, reported another apparition.

As he was in the field, tending to the cattle grazing in one of the fields on the former Keim land, he saw the ghost of a white horse emerge from the tall grass a short distance away. He claims that one cow also saw the phantom steed and dropped dead on the spot.

These kinds of stories are substantiated by some rather high-calibre folks of the Oley Valley social structure. And generally, the old Keim home is considered to be one of Berks County's classic "haunted houses."

While the far-fetched tales of ghost horses and the like may be difficult for even the most imaginative ghost-hunter to believe, the Keim property does have its mysteries, even today.

In the course of researching this book, we spoke with the man who resides in the Keim home today. A dashing figure, he lives the life of a contemporary bachelor, but holds dearly to the heritage of the home he lives in and maintains. His stories about life in the house are abrupt and there is the feeling that he's not ready to "tell all," even to this writer who promised his anonymity. Still, he outlined some of the modern-day oddities about the house, located on a winding back road that itself is somehow ominous and foreboding.

The house, as it stands today, is actually two homes joined together to give the appearance of one. The common wall that runs between the two structures features at one point a door on one side that leads only to what was once the other exterior wall and a window in it. Between the door and window there is virtually no space. Still, one evening while relaxing on the "door side" of the wall, the current resident was shaken by a loud BANG on the OTHER side of the door — the side of the door totally inaccessible.

Strange and unexplainable bumps in the night have been heard, he told me almost matter-of-factly. On windless nights, shutters banged against the window frame.

The man who lives there now is a meticulous housekeeper, and his penchant for neatness gave rise one evening to the feeling that someone, or something, was sharing the premises with him. Obsessed with the feeling that the seams on a lampshade should be turned toward the wall and out of sight, the man did just that after noticing that one of the shades' seams was visible from the living area of the parlor. He did this before leaving for work one morning. But when he came home to the empty house that night, the shade was turned with the seam clearly visible once again!

What's more, the man has a lady friend who came to visit one day, and followed him to the barn to the rear of the house. She walked calmly in the barn, expecting nothing, but stopped suddenly. She quietly, methodically, backed out, telling her friend she had the strangest sensation. Saying that she was "sensitive" to the spiritual world, she affirmed that there was an evil spirit in that barn, and has since refused to enter it.

A FEW MILES across the valley from the Keim homestead lies the often-photographed and extremely picturesque Oley Forge complex, now inhabited by a well-known Reading shopkeeper and his wife. Although the disavow and knowledge of supernatural beings inside the quaintly elegant ironmaster's mansion, the previous owner tells of a haunting that drew respected mediums and even the renowned author Hans Holzer to conclude that the place indeed housed ghosts and was one the most interesting "haunted houses" in the entire United States.

The forge, near Spangsville, was faithfully restored in the late 1960's by Richard H. Shaner, a teacher and historian who brought the property back from the depths of disrepair after decades of decline. The Ironmaster's dwelling was built in the middle of the 18th century and its forge supplied materiel for the Revolutionary War effort. There is a secret passageway in a cliff adjacent to the mansion and evidence that the forge had direct personal connections to Betsy Ross. One of the Forge's three partners was John Ross, uncle of the fabled flag-maker from Philadelphia. The other two partners in the forge were John Yoder and Colonel John Lesher.

But it is the spectral inhabitants we are concerned with, and there are supposedly four of them. Seances and hypnotic sessions inside the home have indicated that the ghostly quartet includes a male servant, a young woman, a large dog and the ironmaster, Col. Lesher.

Shaner, who moved out of the house several years ago, says he has heard a young girl chanting "Twinkle, twinkle, little star . . ." and the whimpering of an unseen dog. More recently, Shaner joined with a professional hypnotist to engage in what is called "historical hypno-sis," where individuals are hypnotized and taken back into time to see and hear their experiences in what may have been their previous lives.

IN THE OLEY VALLEY, there are architectural aberrations that must be pointed out when discussing the supernatural. Several homes and cabins in the valley were equipped with "soul holes" or "soul windows." These holes, built into the walls of the structures, were most prevalent in the homes of the early Moravians who settled in the area, and a fine example may be seen in the Bertolet-Herbein cabin now on the grounds of the Daniel Boone Homestead near Baumstown.

Strict historians differ on the meaning or function of these holes that open from the inside of the homes. In his "Annals of the Oley Valley" (Reading Eagle Press, 1926), the Rev. P. C. Croll mentioned such a hole in the Kauffman house:

In the front bedroom is a small opening through the south wall near the ceiling which was undoubtedly left as a port hole for defense against Indian depradators by the builder.

Perhaps the more titillating, and yes, romantic, explanation for these "soul holes" comes from the practice that gave them their popular names.

It is said that the holes were placed there so that should anyone die inside the house, their body would be taken to the room with the hole, and the hole would be opened to allow the spirit of the deceased to leave the home and find its way to Heaven, or the "other side."

Whatever purpose these "soul holes" really served is left in the dust of time. But, along with the Sacred Oak, the haunted ironmaster's mansion and the many other ghosts and legends of the Oley Valley, they add up to a wonderfully mysterious section of our haunted county.

THE HEADLESS PIGS OF ADAMSTOWN

— Dr. Shoemaker's Columns

The quiet village of Adamstown is surrounded by steep hills and valleys that seem to invite folk tales and legends. But the few streets of this borough that straddles Berks and Lancaster Counties boast their own peculiar stories.

Ghost pigs. Headless ghost pigs. The words are certain to imply the wildest of thoughts. But the story of such creatures has been passed on through Adamstown's history, while few people in the town claim to have seen the spiris of the swine in recent years. The story goes that the castoff grain residue from the former Echtenach distillery in Adamstown was fed to the pigs in the barnyard next door. The pigs would grow fatter, and the butcher would do a marvelous business. But it is also recorded in the not-so-accurate history of Adamstown that there were so many hogs slaughtered there that some people would see the headless ghosts of the animals roaming the streets at night!

Another animal figures prominently in Adamstown ghostlore. Actually, it's nothing more than a little black dog hat has been seen at night. The pup appears as if from nowhere, follows an unsuspecting pedestrian for a short distance, and fades into oblivion.

There are, of course, human-like spirits in Adamstown — at least in the minds of some of the older residents there. They speak of "die weiss fraa un die schwatz fraa," or the white woman and the black woman. The two ghosts, clad in the color dresses that gave them their names, walked the streets of the town and have been seen on particularly dark nights. Anyone bold enough to follow either one of them would be led to the town's cemetery where the mysterious wraiths would disappear.

PHANTOM HITCHHIKERS

— *Various Sources*
August, 1982

Several years ago a cabaret singer named Jerome Alch disappeared while performing at a popular Reading night club. His body was later found along the Pennsylvania Turnpike, but a strange incident occurred between his disappearance and the discovery of his body.

The West Chester local news front-paged a story about the reports of the bizarre happenings on the superhighway — happenings that took place near the spot where workmen found Alch's body.

His body and the wreck of his car were found in the icy waters of the Marsh Creek in Upper Uwchlan Township near the Downingtown interchange of the pike. He had been missing from a singing engagement at the Plaza Madrid in Reading for three weeks. Officials at the scene when his body was found said the 37-year old singer could have been dead that long. No autopsy was ordered.

For those three weeks, there were at least a dozen reports of ghostly sightings and occurrences that took place between the Downingtown and Morgantown interchanges, according to the West Chester newspaper. Motorists observed a spectral hitchhiker along the turnpike, and those brave enough to pick him up were warned of the imminent end of the world. Then, just as mysteriously as the hitchhiker appeared . . . he disappeared!

Similar reports in other locales have been publicized at various other times, and have become a part of what are now called "Urban Legends" by sociologists. But motorists questioned about the turnpike incidents claimed no knowledge of prior stories or of Alch's disappearance. In fact, the ghostly reports were given prior to the finding of his body. Up until the discovery of the wreck nobody had any ideas as to Alch's whereabouts.

Although many reports of the supernatural happenings were made after the finding of Alch's body, and therefore subject to sensationalism, many people naively told their tales — unknowing of any part of the Jerome Alch saga. One woman said she nearly hit a medial strip guard rail when she turned around to see who was tapping her on her shoulder while she was driving — alone!

Others reported seeing an apparently distraught young man standing along the turnpike with hands outstretched toward the heavens and as they drove closer, he faded away into thin air.

As Shirley Macauley, of the Local News staff said, "Perhaps the phantom hitchhiker was the spirit of a man unable to accept the sudden fact of his own death, that he appeared along the roadside seeking help, discovery, confirmation, and that the end of the world he is supposed to have predicted was the end, not of the entire world, but of his own."

The ghostly annals of this area include yet another phantom hitchhiker, of another place and time.

There was a time when a long covered bridge linked the town of Birdsboro with a corner of Exeter Township across the Schuylkill. And, it is at this bridge, many years ago, that an intriguing local legend has its roots.

As a legend, it falls into a familiar form, similar to the Jerome Alch story. But it represents yet another morsel in the supernatural smorgasbord of Berks County.

The approaches to the old wooden bridge have long ago been obscured by underbrush. A concrete and steel span now carries traffic into Birdsboro, less than a mile from its covered counterpart. South Baumstown Road today makes a sharp turn away from the former bridge ramp, and the bridge itself is only a vague memory. But another memory lives in the minds of some of the elders of the area — the memory of the veiled lady of the bridge.

In the days before dusk-to-dawn lighting brightened many a dark corner and speeding automobiles replaced the clip-clop of horses' hooves and the steady whirr of wagon wheels, the mere setting of a covered bridge entrance along a quiet, isolated country road would conjure up certain romantic emotions.

This particular approach to the old Birdsboro bridge, however, has been etched into the local legend ledger thanks to the mysterious woman.

This woman supposedly would beckon buggy drivers, seeking a ride with them across the bridge. But once in the darkened confines of the covered bridge, she would disappear. Some say she said nothing and offered only a forlorn smile, while others say she spoke of the reality of life after death and assured anyone who would listen that a good life spent here on earth would be rewarded in the hereafter.

The bridge is gone, but some folks in the Baumstown area claim the old veiled mystery lady still walks along South Baumstown Road on misty evenings, teasing drivers to continue straight onto the old bridge approach and into the woods that now consume the former roadbed, instead of making the sharp turn that takes them to route 82.

INDIAN LEGENDS, POWWOWING AND EARLY SUPERSTITIONS

— Various Sources

Berks is a very old, established county, with its earliest settlers and Indian natives well represented in its formal history books and folklore. What gives Berks County a distinctly different folklore base, however, is the nature of its first settlers, who brought with them the superstitions and beliefs of their homelands. In this chapter we shall look at some of the more enduring Indian stories and also the rites of "Powwowing" and witchcraft that have contributed to the unique heritage of Berks County.

Indian lore is strongly represented in Berks County history books, and too, the natives of this land figure in the rolls of the supernatural.

The famous story of "Lovers' Leap" is perhaps the most familiar to most of us, while the details and locale of the event may vary, as such information often does in the world of legends. But one version involves Sarah Wynne, a Quaker maiden and Unalach, a handsome Indian brave, who were lovers who could never marry because of the obvious idealogical differences. Sarah's parents most definitely prohibited the affair, but ultimately, their love conquered all.

The despondent lovers hiked to the summit of Neversink Mountain and from a cliff now plainly visible from the West Shore Bypass, leaped to their deaths. At last, they were together.

Another Indian legend brings into play two of the county's most interesting and enigmatic natural phenomena — thickly-forested mountains and caves.

Towkee and Oneeda were Indian lovers. After following accepted tribal procedure, they put the question of marriage before their parents. Much to their sorrow, the answer was "no." They decided they would die together, since life together was out of the question.

They told friends to watch for a flaming dragon, which would fly from the summit of Round Top Mountain to where their bodies would be found. Sure enough, the dragon made its flight and landed at what is now called Dragon Cave in Richmond Township. Their bodies were found in the cave, the part of which has been named the "Temple of the Dragon." Today, supposedly, the dragon can still be seen flying from the mountain top to the cave, and inside the cavern the ghostly moans of the two dead lovers can be heard.

During interviews with residents of the farms and homes around Dragon Cave, I found other versions of the legend. The variations were slight, but at least the people were familiar with the dragon's flight and moans of the lovers.

Some people heard that the dragon flew from nearby Shofer's Cave, not Round Top, and to Dragon Cave. Others heard that the lovers were a white girl and Indian brave. Still others said it was an Indian girl and white boy.

Regardless, the legend has been repeated through the ages and is still as widely known today as, perhaps a century ago.

The ghosts of two more Indian lovers, unable to live together for the rest of their lives, walk the ruins of the former Blue Falls Inn and the grounds around it. The two were fishing along the swift-flowing Maiden Creek when the young woman was bit by a poisonous snake. The young brave frantically sought the one root that was used to heal the snake bite, but could find none. The girl died. The young man, broken-hearted, plunged his hunting knife into his chest and died alongside his lover. The two were buried near a large cypress tree near the site of the mansion, which burned down several years ago. But the two Indians supposedly stroll the grounds of the Blue Falls area after dark, hand in hand, eternally.

Some of Berks County's legendary figures have been honored by historical markers that preserve their memory. One of these markers is found near Hill Church in the majestic hills surrounding the Oley Valley. It marks the site of the home of Anna Maria Jung, the colorful and mysterious "Mountain Mary."

Mary came to America in 1769. Her family settled in Germantown but moved to Oley after the death of Mary's father during the Revolution. In her new home here in Berks County, Mary took a husband. He, too, became a victim of the battlefields and died while serving in the Continental Army.

For years after her husband's death, "Die Berg Maria" lived alone, doling out spiritual and medicinal aid to Indians and whites who often came distances of hundreds of miles to receive her providence.

Although there is considerable evidence that she did not, in fact, partake in powwowing or witchcraft, there is also considerable evidence to the contrary.

Arthur Lewis, in his book, "Hex," calls Mountain Mary "Pennsylvania's most famous witch," and connected an incident in Mountain Mary's life with the subject of the hex murderer, John Blymire. Blymire's grandfather was born on the same day Mary died. According to Andrew Blymire, John's father, the eldest Blymire had a "strange fondness for owls." Mary, troubled by a persistent owl who continually drank milk from her pail as she did the evening milking, caught the bird one night and burned its feet slightly, hopefully to prevent its return. The next morning, a neighbor lady complained that she couldn't put her shoes on because of burned feet.

A close friend of Mary's, Mrs. John Keim, had a vision of Mountain Mary calling for her. She made a trip from Reading to the Oley Hills and found Mary in the final throes of death. She was with her until the end. Mary died in November, 1819. The Daughters of the American Revolution erected a monument in Mary's honor in 1934. It stands at the site of her home near Hill Church.

Most native Berks Countians are somewnat familiar with the art of "powwowing." Even today, some of the old-guard "Dutchmen" still visit powwow doctors before consulting a physician in even the gravest matters of health. These faith-healers and "witches" practice necromancy in urban and rural Berks, Lancaster and York counties. Interestingly, as a sidebar, it can be noted that similar practices are carried on by the large Hispanic population of Berks County, many of whom brought with them the strange "voodoo" of the Caribbean islands.

But the good, old-fashioned powwowers of Berks are still at it, and still consult such manuals as "The Long Lost Friend," the powwowers medical textbook, or the "Sixth and Seventh Books of Moses," another must for the powwowers library. For the benefit of students of the Bible, these sixth and seventh books do not appear in the testaments, but were taken from the mosaic books of the Cabala and the Talmud.

"The Long Lost Friend," or "Der Lang Verbogen Freund," was written by John George Hohman and made its bow on the literary scene in 1819. It was printed in Reading and contained 84 pages. About a half-million copies of this book have been repinted in 150 editions. Reprints of it are available today, but few original first editions remain.

Hohman promised the reader, ". . . whosoever carries this book with him would be protected from drowning, burning and would avoid any unjust sentence passed upon him."

Hohman further offered dozens of cures and remedies that would relieve the reader of virtually ever ailment known to man. For instance — for a toothache, prick your afflicted tooth with a needle until it bleeds, take a thread and soak it with blood. Then take vinegar and flour, mix them into a paste and spread some of the goo on a cloth. Wrap the cloth around the root of an apple tree and tie it lightly with the blood-soaked thread. Then, cover the root with soil. The toothache will subside.

For hens that aren't laying, simply get some rabbit dung, mash it into a fine powder, mix it with bran, wet it until it lumps and feed it to the hens. Many eggs will follow.

To cure epilepsy, Hohman offered this: Cut the throat of a turtle dove and have the epileptic drink its blood.

To protect yourself from all injuries, Hohman said, carry the right eye of a wolf fastened inside your right sleeve.

To cure warts, roast chicken feet and rub them on the warts. Then, bury the feet under the eaves of your house.

Birth and death are addressed in the world of powwowing. There are suggested ways to stave off various birth defects and hereditary personality traits.

Quite honestly, I have a strange compulsion to smell things. I feel the need to take a whiff of anything that passes my way. My favorite smells are the pages in a new book, new wallets, cold newspapers, and many other things.

My mother worked for several months while she was carrying me. One of her bosses at the northern Berks knitting mill in which she was employed was also a compulsive sniffer. He would enter the mill and sniff around, his nose always seeking a new thrill. My mother, along with several other young women in his employ, noticed this oddity and it became a focal point for conversation and mild jesting throughout the mill.

One day an old philosopher-housewife told my mother, "If you criticize somebody's peculiarity while you're pregnant, your child will inherit the same peculiarity."

And, although it is seemingly unexplainable, unbelievable and medically unlikely, I am living proof that compulsive sniffing is a communicable hereditary disorder!

Another strange tale comes from northern Berks, near Bethel. The old adage says that if a woman is scared by a mouse during her pregnancy the baby will be born with a hairy birthmark. This apparently came true in the case of one man. His mother can distinctly remember being frightened nearly out of her wits by a mouse one day. Her baby boy was born with a very distinct mouseshaped, hairy birthmark.

If a pregnant woman stoops to go under a fence, the baby will be stillborn, with its umbilical cord causing death by strangulation.

One more superstition based upon the ancient powwowing theories professes that if the first shirt a baby wears is taken off inside out, the baby will be immune to whopping cough.

Do not tickle a child before he becomes one year old and he'll not stammer. Also, if rain falls upon a child's face, he or she will have freckles. To prevent freckles, wash his or her face in the early morning dew.

To ensure good luck for a child, do not cut an infant's fingernails, bite them off. For even better luck, always burn the baby's first diaper.

In less enlightened times, left-handedness was thought to be the product of the Devil, so the powwow manuals included two precautionary measures that should make the child a "righty." One, when the baby dons his or her first clothing, the right sleeve should be worn first. And, if you nurse the infant with the right breast first, it will be right-handed.

Turning from cures and such, we will now examine the Berks County way of death. Many omens and superstitions surround the "facts of death" hereabous.

Many signs warn of impending death. According to superstition, if a cricket enters the house, there will be a death in the family. Other omens include: if a dog whines while under a window; if someone sneezes at the dinner table, and if horses neigh at a funeral.

If thirteen people sit down to a meal, one will die within one year's time. If you smell the flowers on a grave, your sense of smell may be destroyed.

"If you sing before breakfast, you'll cry berore supper" is another widely known adage. A woman from northwestern Berks had a tragic experience with this proverb.

In 1988, when the woman was a young girl, she came to the breakfast table singing merrily. Her mother, an old-line Pennsylvania "Dutchman," admonished the girl. "Don't sing before breakfast, you'll cry before supper!" The youngster lightly brushed the old wives' tale aside, but stopped singing to please her mother.

After breakfast, the girl rushed off to school. Her mother's warning was virtually forgotten during the day, but when the school day ended, the mother's manticism was to bear shocking and tragic results.

Still in a jovial mood, the young girl came skipping to the big house, happily singing the melody that brought the maternal warning earlier that day.

"I'm home, Mom," said the little girl as she entered the front door. There was a grave silence. Perhaps her mother was in the backyard. The girl ran around back, finding only the stationary outhouse and a maze of washline suspended from wooden poles. The only other alternative was that her mother was asleep in her upstairs sewing room.

The girl proceeded back inside, calling for her mother. Upstairs, she was to finally find her mom. As the youngster stood at the doorway of the sewing room she was indeed gratified to see her mother, soundly sleeping.

Since the little girl knew her mother would soon have to awaken from her nap to fix supper for the family, she walked into the room to arouse her slumbering parent. But, to her horror, her mother could not be awakened. She had fallen into an eternal sleep.

The little girl cried.

THE GHOST AT GRING'S MILL

— Various Sources
August, 1982

One needn't have a ghost-hunter's imagination to feel the eerie atmosphere of a lonely canal towpath at midnight on a dank, foggy, rainy night.

Raindrops pelted the soft soil and thumped a rhythmic pattern imitating muted footsteps. The glow from distant roadside lamps cast a luminescent glow of the wet leaves and slick mosses in the deep, empty canal bed.

The small, nocturnal search party had come to seek the ghosts of Mrs. Phillip Bissinger and her three children, Mollie, Lillie and Phillip, who met a tragic and untimely death in lock #49 of the Union Canal at about 5 p.m., August 17, 1875.

The Bissinger family was well-known and well-liked, and the resultant suicide and triple-murder carried out by Louisa Bissinger shocked the entire Reading community and sparked one of the most bizarre scandals in the city's history.

Contemporary newspaper articles chronicled the events of the fateful evening of August 17th, but wild speculation was all that was offered as a reason for what the young woman did. Some said Louisa was insane — others hinted that she had become aware of an affair her husband was having. Her motives for suicide, and taking her three children with her, remain locked inside her soul.

At about 2 p.m. on her final day of life, Mrs. Bissinger, who was pregnant, left on a trolley car with her three children and went to the northwestern terminus of the trolley line. From there, the ill-fated quartet continued over the Lebanon Valley Railroad Bridge and on toward the farm of Charles Gring, following the Union Canal towpath. Along the way, Louisa had her children gather stones and place them in baskets she carried. In their innocence, the children had no way of knowing they were collecting the stones that would carry them to their watery graves. A Coroner's Jury later determined that twenty-one pounds of stones were gathered, and the baskets lashed around the mother's waist with a heavy cord.

One person who claimed to meet the woman and her children along the towpath at about four o'clock that afternoon said she was in good spirits. About an hour later, however, the woman clutched her children, held them tight, and leaped into the seven-feet deep canal lock. Neither Louisa nor her three children could swim, and the heavy stones helped them sink quickly to the bottom. The children screamed as they knew what was happening, and a man named William Behm heard the frantic cries of the children and ran to the scene to help — but Behm was also a non-swimmer. By the time he arrived at the lock, the last gasp of bubbles were rising to the surface. The mother and children had drowned.

The bodies were retrieved and Deputy Coroner Goodhart was summoned to the farmhouse at Gring's Mill. The corpses were laid out on the front porch of the farmhouse until a wagon arrived to transport them to the E. S. Miller Funeral Home at 420 Washington Street in Reading. A neighbor of the Bissingers made the positive identification of the victims, and Mr. Bissinger was contacted at the Harmonie Maennerchor rehearsal at Liberty Hall and given the bad news. He broke down, and an account of the ordeal reveals that he was so distraught that "opiates were used to calm him."

The newspaper articles of the day were graphic in their description of the corpses as they lay in the funeral home:

. . . the appearance of Mrs. Bissinger was considerably changed. Her face was broad and puffed up, although her features could be distinctly traced. The little children looked very natural, but the sparkle of their black, lustrous eyes was gone, as they lay in their narrow coffins, cold and lifeless corpses.

The vivid accounts of the Bissinger tragedy resulted in the sale of 7,500 copies of the Reading EAGLE the next day, a new single sale unprecedented in Reading journalistic history.

In addition, angry letters from Bissinger family members showed up in subsequent issues, and a book detailing the tragedy appeared in shops within weeks after the ordeal.

Today, the Bissinger tragedy is just another strange story from Reading and Berks County's past. It is interesting to note, though, that the county Park and Recreation Department remembers the horror of August 17, 1875 in its "Union Canal Towpath Tour" brochure distributed at Gring's Mill Park. The mention of the event is preceded with a warning: "If you happen to wander out here late some night be on guard for the ghost of Mrs. Phillip Bissinger . . ."

It was very late one night when this writer and three reporters from the Reading Eagle-Times ventured onto the towpath looking for the Bissinger ghosts. We kept our appointed rendezvous despite a steady rainfall and chilly temperatures. Trudging along the towpath from the dambreast near the Gring farmhouse to lock #49 and beyond, we saw no ghostly shapes or forms. As the story of the Bissinger tragedy was retold, along with other local ghost stories, we wondered aloud what would happen if we were to have an actual encounter with a ghost.

We walked back toward our cars, shoulders drooping from the lack of success. We came to a spot directly in front of the Gring house when one of the reporters stopped suddenly. He clutched his chest, leaned against a stump and gasped for air. His words were fragmented, as if an unseen force had actually entered his body. It was a scene none of us had ever witnessed before. This particular young man was not given to making a spectacle of himself. Any such behavior was more than likely genuine. We gathered at his side to help, if we could, but within seconds he regained his senses. Still, he was unable to describe the feeling that overtook him. He, too, had never encountered anything like it in his life!

Was this a kind of warning? Was it actually the attempt by a spirit to enter the body of this reporter? To this day, each of us who witnessed the event remains puzzled.

The story of the ghost(s) at Gring's Mill takes a strange twist when new information is added to it. Information not from Gring's farmhouse or lock #49, but from the former Althouse mansion directly across the Tulpehocken Creek from the Gring house.

The sprawling Althouse property was the home of a wealthy Reading industrialist, but more recently was acquired by a nationally-known insurance firm. For several years, the company maintained offices in the former Althouse mansion, but went on to build a magnificent office building on a part of the land along the Bernville Road.

It was while the firm did business from the old mansion that the next ghost story was born. Two women, employees of the insurance firm, reported seeing the figure of a rotund, smallish gentlemen at the foot of a spiral staircase in the main lobby of the home. They were working at their desks, and looked up to see the apparition. The man, middle-aged and well-dressed, as the women recall, just turned and disappeared up the steps. This same basic encounter was made on two separate occasions.

As might be expected, the two women became the center of conversation after they nervously revealed their sightings to their fellow workers. And while their compatriots chuckle a bit when the story is told, they know the women well enough to feel that yes, indeed, they did see somebody — something — that they could not explain.

HISTORY AND MYSTERY

— *Various Sources*
August, 1982

So many of the ghost stories collected in our search for the supernatural lack any substantive form, and are difficult to "stand alone." Thus, in this chapter we will look at some bits and pieces of tales as told along the way to the completion of this book.

What could be one of the more fascinating ghost stories to spring from the fact or fancy of a Berks Countian has been, for all intents and purposes, lost forever to a severe case of the storyteller's craving for total anonymity.

What remains of the potentially interesting tale is only a skeletal sketch — a tidbit of temptation for the mind's savoring.

The story is passed on from one of the county's most respected historians and research librarians. Her memory of the incident which occurred in the mid-1960's is clouded by time's passage and this writer's recollection of the casual conversation which led to the tale's telling may have further tilted the facts. But be assured, the story is generally accurate.

The routine of life within the offices and research rooms of the Historical Society of Berks County was broken that day several years ago when, through the door of the venerable vault of our heritage walked a young girl and her mother, sheepishly approaching anyone who would or could satisfy their somewhat unorthodox query.

Without elaborating on the matter, and without specifically stating a reason for such divulgence, the two asked if they might see a painting, sketch or rendering of a Hessian soldier — the enlisted man's uniform that may very well have been in abundant view during the Revolutionary War period in which the town of Reading was the site of a large prisoner-of-war camp.

The visitors' interest in the merceneries' vestments was not purely historical. Those Historical Society staff members present could readily detect an underlying anxiety beneath the forced calm of the inquiry. As any available visual documentation of the Hessian uniform was sought in the society's vast collections, the reason for the ladies' request was divulged. The revelation sent shivers through the nervous systems of those present, as the roots of mystery sank through the soil of imagination, only to quickly wither in the garden of anonymity.

About all that could be ascertained about the visitors that day is that they were visibly shaken by their experience and that they resided somewhere on the perimeter of Neversink Mountain. Their reason for seeking information on a Hessian's uniform was then to become a cruel tease for this ghost hunter!

Perhaps, they thought, a look at a documented representation of a Hessian soldier, circa 1778, would unlock the doors of the personal nightmare the two had shared for many months. Perhaps the spectre they had seen inside their home on several occasions was that of a Hessian soldier who met his date with destiny along the slopes of Neversink. The ghost that had walked into their home, wearing a strange uniform may be historically verifiable.

Only speculation can fill in the wide gaps of truth or fiction conjured up by the incident. No amount of subtle coaxing could convince the pair who visited the society that day to sign the visitors' register on the receptionist's desk. Therefore, no record was to be made regarding the idenity of the mother and daughter. All that is, and likely will ever be known about "Hessian Ghost" is a mere framework of what could be a tantalizing tale of spectral visitation.

Also in the Historical Society's collection is a stunning painting of a young girl, possessed with an innocent face and pose. The simplicity of the portrait belies the details of the story behind it.

Earlier in this century, a young mother was in the parlor of her home, occupying herself while her young daughter slept in an upstairs bedroom. A strange sensation consumed the woman and, as if from nowhere, the vision of a spritely-dressed, cherubic child glided down the staircase. As the vision faded, the woman put down her labors and proceeded, solemnly, to her daughter's bedroom with the full knowledge of what she would find. Her little girl was dead.

Following the burial and mourning period, the woman commissioned an artist to paint, from her vivid description, a portrait of this vision. That portrait has since found its way into the collection of the Historical Society.

From northeast Reading comes a true story told by a Perry Street woman named Carol.

Carol's husband was away for the night on a business trip, and against his better wishes, Carol elected to stay home alone in the big rowhome, rather than spend the night with her parents as she did on other similar occasions. As you shall see, after the spine-chilling night she experienced, Carol doubtlessly wishes she had gone home to Mom and Dad!

She was listening to a hushed stereo, paging through a magazine and quietly biding her time before retiring for the evening. Her solitude was suddenly shattered by a voice from another room.

"James . . . JAMES!" The voice was of a young woman and was

definitely coming from the dining room of Carol's home. Her attention was swept to this clear and spectral voice — her ears perked as the voice continued:

"No, please, James!"

Carol was certain that the voice was not filtering through the common wall from an adjoining house. No, she knew the plaintive call was from the dining room. From her vantage point, she could see all but a corner of the dining room and frozen momentarily by fear, she broke the grip and with her heart pounding and jaw shaking peeked around for a full view of the dining room. A strange relief warmed her when she saw nothing or no one in the room. But the icy fingers of terror crawled over her again when a terrifying, ghostly moan sliced the silence. Carol sought the refuge of the front door as she witnessed a brilliant flash of bluish-green light in the dining room. Surely she was going mad, or dreaming. She knew in her heart, however, that what she was hearing and seeing was all too real. Carol called a neighbor over for security and assurance, but would not tell her of the experience she just had. She explained her nervousness as the result of a television show she was watching.

Carol lived with her secret until the night she related it to her hsuband, and later to this writer. Her husband scoffs it off as her "imagination running wild," but Carol keeps her ghostly encounter hidden deeply in her memory. Only she knows what happened that night, and nobody at this point can tell if the simple rowhome in northeast Reading — a house which she and her husband have moved away from — is really haunted!

Across town, a story has lingered for the better part of the 20th century — the story of the ghost of Clover Alley. This narrow alley, between Moss and 10th Streets, was the site of a murder sometime around the turn of the century. The story follows familiar form, a lover's triangle resulting in the murder of an unfaithful wife by the jealous husband. The exact location of the home involved has been forgotten, but it is recorded in previously-published stories that neighbors heard "wails and groans eminating from the house," and "Mrs. Ruppert," who lived nearby, claimed to see the headless figure of a woman dressed in black walk through the gate leading to the house in which the murder took place. Reportedly, the victim was buried in Leesport and the murderer eventually interred in an Alsace Township cemetery. Folks living near the Alsace graveyard later said they heard a woman's voice calling in the night, "Oh, Harry . . . Oh, Harry" wafting through the tombstones.

Near the Central Catholic High School stadium in the borough of St. Lawrence, there was an old farmhouse where, sometime in the 1960's a passerby reported seeing what they described as "a fiery man running up a tree." Others claim to have seen fiery dogs on the same property.

A Robesonia woman swears to the following events: It all started innocently enough, with hanging plants gently swaying on a breeze-less day; the seemingly unprovoked barking of the dog; the familiar aroma of cigar smoke.

The widow eventually recognized the cigar smoke as that of her late husband's, and one night actually saw her deceased loved one walk into the living room, fully dressed except for his shoes, which he was carrying. Her love for him overcame the fear of the moment, and she walked over to embrace his returning spirit, only to watch it vanish as she drew closer.

The same situation was repeated several times, and the woman contacted a card reader who advised her to help her husband find the way to the other side. "The next time his spirit visits you," she said, "repeat three times 'Norman, you are dead — leave me alone!'" This would at once relieve her anguish and send her husband's confused spirit to the light.

Sure enough, within days the spirit returned. The woman gathered her senses and did what had to be done.

Just after the third recitation, the spirit faded away and never returned!

Near the village of Grill is an old riding stable that at one time was a very exclusive place. The playful mannerisms of the bachelor who once owned the facility may contribute to some of the unexplainable events that have taken place there. These events continued from the 50s into the 60s, and baffled everyone from riding instructors to studens to the horses themselves.

At one point in the corral, instructors noticed that horses would fall for no apparent reason. Describing their falls, the eye witness made a sweep of her hand to show that it appeared that some mysterious force was knocking the horses' legs from under them.

Others recall that some horses simply refused to walk into that particular section of the ring. Some steeds, trotting calmly in other parts of the ring, spooked when they reached the affected area.

Our storyteller's theory? She recalls that the prior owner of the stable was a prankster, and feels that his spirit may haunt the corral, playing tricks on the horses.

In the mid-70s, three Kutztown State College coeds met the spirit of a woman who supposedly died in a home on Whiteoak Street. They say a mirror, anchored firmly to a bedroom wall, literally leaped from the wall and fell violently on the floor in the middle of the night. Weird noises and bumps were heard in the wee small hours. On one occasion, while the girls were photographing each other in the living room of the home, a strange face-like vision showed up, appearing as if it was peering through a window. This writer saw these photographs and is still pondering their authenticity.

Still in Kutztown, there is a story known to most freshmen girls at Kutztown State — the story of the ghost of "Old Main." The campus' central building along Main Street is said to be haunted by the spirit of a freshman girl who died inside. A wild story designed to strike fear at the hearts of frosh? Perhaps, but who knows?

The site of "Fingal's Castle," an incredible estate built by a French prince during the French and Indian War, is somewhere near Morgantown. While hikers and southern Berks historians claim to know the actual site, virtually all vestiges of the castle, gardens, outbuildings and horse track have disappeared. But the ghost of Fingal, whoever he may have been, still walks through the thick brush of what was once his domain.

Northeast Reading is haunted by at least two spirits. One young woman who walks along the ridge of the Hampden Reservoir, and has been seen by a city police officer. He saye he saw the figure, wearing an ankle-length dress, slowly walking across the rim of the basin, silhouetted in the early-morning sky. He drove his car up the winding road leading him closer to her. As he approached, the figure became less clear and slowly faded away to nothing. The officer stopped his car, shook and scratched his head, and thought about reporting the incident to the radio dispatcher. He thought again, and realized he'd be better off just keeping it to himself!

Another restless spirit is said to wander through the sand quarry near McKnight's Gap. A Reading businessman whose business and personal lives had gone sour, committed suicide in the quarry, and to this day haunts the quarry.

The quest for buried treasure somewhere in the Monocacy area has recurred throughout published accounts over the last century. One story reveals a wild search for the booty, randomly estimated at from $30,000 to $300,000, stashed away by an unknown person or persons on what was delineated as the "Charles Tracey farm" near that southern Berks community. For our purposes, this story becomes fascinating when it is divulged that the treasure-hunters of 1901 were led to the area by a local man reported seeing the ghost of a French Huguenot settler who returned to advise him of the location of the treasure. The man substantiated the spirit's claim by hiring a Pottstown powwower to accompany him to the general area and offer an independent analysis of the situation. The powwower confirmed that there was a quantity of gold buried somewhere on the property.

By all indications, the treasure was never recovered, and if the word of a bearded Huguenot ghost can be believed, a great sum of gold still lies untouched, deep in the soil somewhere near Monocacy!

There are many, many more stories of the unexplained here in Berks County — the albino ape-like creature of Bethel Township, the legend of the "dog woman" of northwestern Berks, the elusive light near Fritztown, the swinging lamp that glows on and off in the Dreibelbis Bridge, the heavy-breathing, creaking floorboards and poltergeistic activities in a Walnuttown home, the headless ghost said to walk through the hamlet of Gibraltar — so many more stories that have baffled and frightened Berks Countians through the years. No single volume such as this could ever do justice to all of of them.

THE AMBER LIGHT CIRCLE

— Personal Research
August, 1982

The following stories purport to demonstrate a mortal's ability to help a repentant or grieving spirit find peace on "the other side."

It is interesting to know that variations on such a theory are common amongst those who are true believers in the spiritual world. Within Berks County, at the time of this writing, there is a kind of spiritual support group that delves into this practice of seeking out troubled and confused spirits and sending them to "the light" through a little bit of incantation, and a lot of basic faith and love.

This "Amber Light Circle," as the group calls itself, meets weekly in a typical suburban home just north of Reading. Its members are from all sectors of the population, including housewives, millworkers, teenagers, senior citizens, professional men and women and others. These meetings are not particularly "mystical" in any way. There are no bizarre light or sound effects, no esoteric symbols of the occult. There is no mind-bending music filtering through hushed ghostly gibberish. These are average people, sitting in a circle in an average recreation room, discussing their common bond and eventually joining together in a hand-holding circle where this faith and love shines through. A self-styled medium acts as an intermediary in a simple but stirring ritual.

This rite, and the bond the participants in the Amber Light Circle all share can never really be understood or penetrated by an outsider. What these people share is simple and profound: Each has witnessed the return of a deceased person. Each has seen a ghost.

The stories vary. Most have encountered departed loved ones — family and friends. They speak of visions of dead sons and daughters, mothers and fathers who appear to them — speak to them. Their stories are impassioned revelations of most private moments spent with the spirits of these people who were, in life, most precious to them. Listening to the stories, one can hardly doubt their sincerity and authenticity. It is a treasure trove of ghost stories, but each so intimate that to tell them here would be a rude invasion of privacy. To the people of the Circle, these stories are far more abstruse than simple "ghost stories," and while the listener may tingle with the sensation of the supernatural, the teller speaks with conviction and the full knowledge that the meeting with the departed loved one has been merely an extension of the love shared when they were alive.

Beyond this connection each person shares, the Amber Light Circle also engages in a kind of faith-healing. That's probably a term shabbily misued in this case, but the "healing circle" phase of an Amber Light meeting certainly must fall somewhere within its definition.

As noted before, the Circle depends almost entirely on love and faith as the strong cord binding each of the members together. These emotions are funneled through a medium who enters a trance-like state of mind as all join together, hand-in-hand, in a gently-swaying, serene "healing circle." With unabashed openness, each participant is asked to cite their physical problems, with each malady or ailment tended to by comforting words and gestures from the medium. Others join as "healers," and seem to be entrusted with the powers to soothe. Prayers are also offered for family members and friends — alive and deceased. And suddenly, a troubled spirit — one which has not yet been shown "the light" — is introduced.

It is that of a young girl named Kelly, killed in an automobile accident and unable to find her way to the other side. The group remains in a circle, still swaying and holding hands. To this casual observer, it is a time of reckoning. To the veterans of the Amber Light Circle, it is a call for action.

The spirit is called upon to enter the circle. She, Kelly, does so. She is introduced to another young spirit who has been asked on other occasions to guide children to a peaceful rest. The group speaks with reassuring bits of spontaneous conversation. They gain the confidence of the little spirit and the task is completed. Kelly is transported from her troubled purgatory to the other side.

Allow this quote from a piece of literature distributed discriminately by the organizer of the Amber Light Circle. Perhaps in its words, the mood of the group may be better defined:

"The Amber Light Circle consists of people like you and me who reach within themselves for the love and light to flow out to others, and to be set free. It's a learning and a sharing of God and Christ within. It's a glowing of love and light we feel and see for all others as well as for you and me. It heals, it strengthens us all."

The lunatic fringe?

Hardly. The credibility of members of the Circle may be questioned, and in fact they welcome such skepticism. Their honesty is strong enough to meet and conquer any doubting Thomases who challenge them. That same honesty, and the matter-of-fact approach to their unique albeit offbeat "talents" would shake some of the doubt from anyone willing to at least keep an open mind toward their stories and methods.

I speak from personal experience on this matter. Entering the meeting place, I was greeted by the members of the Circle. I expected a dimly-lit room and eccentric individuals gathered around or surrounded by strange icons and idols. I found quite normal folk, eager to offer soda and snack foods served from a beer sign and souvenir-bedecked bar in a cozy den that shares the home's basement with a well-stocked workshop. I still approached the people cautiously, expecting something that never materialized. We sat in a circle and discussed my skepticism/open mind concept and their personal experiences. I made no attempts to disguise my suspicions and they made no attempts to rationalize their encounters with spirits, other than to say, in essence, "this is what happened — I know it's hard to believe — but it happened!"

I asked one young woman what brought her to the circle. She smiled innocently and said, "Well, before I tell you, may I let you know that there is a spirit standing right behind you?" Goosebumps surfaced on my skin and the distinct feeling we've all had that someone is looking over our shoulder started to well up inside. I slowly turned around and, of course, saw nothing, er, nobody there. The young woman shrugged and chuckled with an "oh, well, what can I say?" attitude. The rest of the gathering giggled and I sat, head affixed straightforward, absorbing the woman's story. This spirit standing in back of me later disappeared, and there was a feeble attempt made to determine if it was someone following me or just an interested interloper. For some reason, I felt I might rather not know!

Now then, on to the stories of two ghosts sent happily on their way by living persons. The first is set in Birdsboro, many years ago, where a rich, young woman and her dentist husband had just settled into marriage when the bride was killed in a fire at their home. The husband explained to investigators that when they awoke to the smell of smoke and the realization that their home was ablaze, they agreed quickly that he would leap from a second-floor bedroom window and wait for her to jump into his arms. He jumped, but within seconds, the floor of the bedroom collapsed and the woman was burned to death.

While the young woman was wealthy, it was noted that she was not particularly beautiful. In fact the handsome young dentist, who was struggling to establish his practice, was suspected from the beginning of marrying her only for her money.

Those suspicions grew when the widower mysteriously disappeared almost immediately following the fatal fire, with the young woman's fortune withdrawn from the town bank.

As the time passed, the rubble of the fire-ravaged home was cleared, but memories of the fire were not stricken from townspeople.

One night, a passerby reported seeing the form of a woman, dressed in white, rise from the ground where the house once stood. He said she was carrying a brightly-burning lamp and followed him for a short distance. More reports of this same apparition followed and eventually folks tried to avoid this haunted place. But some more daring young men, determined to debunk the ghost stories, went there one moonless midnight. The spirit rose from the lost and glowed eerily in the dark. To their horror, the young men noticed that her left hand had been severed at the wrist. In her right hand, she carried the severed dismembered hand. She reached out to the young men and dropped a piece of paper in front of them. When the paper hit the ground, the spirit vanished.

Trying to sort out what had happened, the young men hurried home with the paper. They gathered around a dim light and unfolded the paper. They felt a sensation surge through their body unlike any other feeling they'd ever experience. What the ghost had handed them was a letter:

I am the spirit of the dentist's wife and have for months and months walked the site of my former habitation for the purpose of finding someone to convey my message to you. Some time before the fire through which my earthly existence was ended for the time being, my husband demanded huge sums of money from me that I would not give. Outwardly he appeared like a saint, but his heart was dark. On the night of the fire he tied me on the bed with a rope and then set the house on fire. After it was already burning, he returned and in his haste to get the diamond ring on my left hand, took a hatchet he had with him and cut off that hand. After I was buried with my goods turned into money, he left for the West. His crime was the cause of his own death. He was killed nine months after his crime by a party of robbers, while fighting for his stolen money. I could find no rest with this terrible man's great crime unrevealed. Now I can rest in Peace.

Another case where the action of a mortal led to the freedom of a troubled spirit took place in Longswamp Township.

The old house along a back road was vacant for years, and was naturally given the monicker of "haunted" by those who tend to label any old, vacant house as such. There was evidence that the house did have its idiosyncracies — creaking floors and steps, a rattling sound in the basement, etc. Because of the "haunted" rumor, though, the owner of the place was hard-pressed to rent it out.

Finally, a poor family agreed to rent the house, ghosts and all. They had been assured by a local soothsayer that any spooks inside were probably "white spirits," as opposed to "black spirits." These references were of behavioral, not racial terms. Whatever, the family was unperturbed, and the first few months of their experience in their new residence were uneventful.

One night, as the family slept, a rattling sound was heard and the father awoke, prepared to investigate. He remembered that the old woman who described the white and black spirits also said that if any spirit appeared, he should have the oldest daughter of the family perform a simple ritual.

He awakened his oldest daughter and followed the directions. She was to wrap her hand in a thick cloth, and if the ghost appeared, ask, "Vas is dei begeear?" (What is it you wish?) Then, if the ghost offered its hand to her, she was to respond in kind.

The girl agreed, and within a few minutes, the rattling sound came closer. A spirit manifested itself, and the girl cautiously went through with what she was instructed.

"Vas is dei begeear?" asked the girl, as the spirit extended its right hand toward her.

The ghost spoke: "I am happy to have you ask me what it is that I wish. These many years I have waited for this moment." The ghost asked the girl to follow it to the cellar. Staggered by the events of the night, the father, daughter and ghost walked downstairs. Again the spirit spoke: "Pull that stone out of the wall and there you will find a copper box. It and everything in it shall be yours. Now my weary wandering is ended. Peace is mine at last!" With those words, the spirit faded and disappeared.

The girl pulled the copper box from the wall, as the ghost had told her. Inside, to everyone's amazement, was an ample supply of gold.

The family was no longer poor.

The house was no longer haunted.

The ghost could finally rest in peace.

THE 27 GHOSTS OF PIG HILL

—Personal Research
August, 1982

Gus. Born September 12, 1764, died October 17. 1864.
Alice. Born November 30, 1771, died August 2, 1835.
Nancy. Born June 13, 1798, died December 31, 1864.

These three people are part of a cast of characters which includes, but is not limited to, Kate and Charles and Otto and Franklin and James and Josephine and a few more ladies and gentlemen who all live happily (most of the time) together in an old home in a Berks County crossroads community known as Pig Hill, or "Sei Baerrick."

And oh yes — I'd better point out that Gus and Alice and the others are the guests of Gene and Mary, the only LIVING inhabitants of the roomy former tavern, hotel, post office, and domicile converted into a full-time home by the mortals who bought it in the mid-1970s.

Gene and Mary fell in love with the place the minute they stepped inside. Oh, it was in sad shape and in need of much repair when it was auctioned. In fact, it was in fairly decrepit shape. But Gene knew his handymanship could whip the massive building into good condition with some tender, loving care and a lot of elbow grease. Gene and Mary also knew, however, that the property would probably draw bids far beyond their means and their dreams would be shattered by financial realtiy.

Still, they wandered throughout the place on auction day, looking beyond the rotting floorboards and beams, crumbling plaster and other signs of deterioration. They envisioned a home restored to the magnificence it must have had when built in 1812.

The couple particularly took note of the deep window sills, walk-in fireplace and the superb features built into every room and hallway. There was no central heating system, and the plumbing and electrical systems were primitive.

As they noted these conditions, however, they also mused that because of its sad shape, the house may sell for less than they thought.

This is exactly what happened, and when the auctioneer's gavel sounded, the house belonged to Gene and Mary.

All repairs, rebuilding and remodeling went quickly and smoothly, for the most part. Within months, the building became a home, and Gene and Mary settled in to enjoy it.

"And enjoy we did," Mary says, "soaking up the peaceful atmosphere of our grand old Dowager, as I'd come to think of the house. Big as she was, her spacious rooms seemed full of the 167 years of living that they had seen. We wondered about the various people who had lived here; they must have loved her as we did. What stories she could tell if only she could speak, stories about her original owners back in 1812, and about the years when she served as a tavern and a store. So many human dramas must have been played out under her roof."

If Mary's words sound precise and measured, it is because they are taken from a voluminous diary in which she recorded the events of the first few months of their lives in the "grand old dowager" of Pig Hill.

If her sentiment toward the old place gives the impression that she wishes "the walls could speak," it is a correct impression. And within a short time Mary and Gene would realize that they would come close to having that wish come true!

"The routine pattern of our lives was short-lived," Mary continues in her diary. "We gradually became aware of unexplainable occurrences. The kitchen light would be on when we came down in the morning. The door leading to the back room behind our bedroom would be open when we went up to change after returning home in the afternoon. The cellar door at the end of the downstairs hall would be standing wide open at almost anytime."

These ominous but probably explainable events were written off as carelessness or forgetfulness. Mary and Gene would kid each other, building a facade to conceal deep feelings both shared about what was actually going on. This facade stood until one evening Gene announced that he thought that something was awry. Gene is a serious, contemplative man, not prone to wild speculation or pranks. Knowing this, Mary felt that he was really concerned. Still, she was skeptical.

Mary finally made her feelings known: "I finally concluded that the only explanation was that we had a ghost."

"A ghost. I'd hardly uttered the words before my intellect told me how absurd the idea was. But somehow, my inner feelings prevailed; somehow I knew I was right, in spite of my better judgement. It was obvious from Gene's calm acceptance of my announcement that he had reached this conclusion sometime ago. He was simply waiting for me to come to it by myself."

From that moment on, their lives were changed. They immediately agreed to double-check each other's goings on. They made certain they had lights turned on and off, doors opened or closed, etc.

This new program of self-monitoring reaped its benefits. One evening, Gene and Mary's daughter dropped by for a visit, eager to hear about their suspicions that the house was the home for a spirit. The young woman casually walked to the kitchen for a drink and remarked that the cellar door was open. Mary relates, "Our hearts skipped beats; this was the first time that we could be absolutely certain that no visible occupant of the house had been near the door for almost 24 hours. We closed it and returned to the livingroom. About an hour passed, an hour filled with excited speculation. I went out to the kitchen to make coffee. As I passed through the hall, I glanced back at the door. Still closed. But ten minutes later, when I returned with the coffee, it was wide open! Again we closed it, but again within an hour it opened."

Mary and Gene wondered about the activity. Would the spirit continue to play these interesting but simple tricks on them, or would it materialize someday? "Just then," Mary writes, "I felt a cool sensation against my side. It was distinct but short-lived, as if some presence had stopped for a moment before continuing on its way. I knew I'd felt something, and thought it wasn't a chill, it was cool. Perhaps it was our ghost."

They triple-checked themselves. The cellar door could not "open by itself" under any circumstances. With the thumb latch secured, as it was in each occasion, there was no way it could open without aid.

Soon, other doors opened mysteriously. "Our unseen friend was obviously enjoying himself and having some fun with us," Mary mused. A muffled tapping sound was heard in the basement. Other noises and bumps were heard. Gene and Mary decided to sit down and try to rationalize their experiences up to this point. It was at this point that Mary decided, too, to begin a diary of the strange events.

"We must have talked until two o'clock that morning, just reliving each experience. We went over every detail. The evidence was certainly mounting. We had something — a presence, a ghost, a spirit, call it what we would, in this grand old house. The idea appealed to us enormously. Although we had never really talked about it, we knew that such a thing was within the realm of possibility. Others had reported the presence of spirits in dwellings. The possibility that our lovely old place sheltered one simply added to our pleasure in the house."

Gene and Mary concluded that whoever was haunting their house was friendly, happy to be there and happy that Gene and Mary were there. They felt that the ghost loved the place as they did.

The supernatural experiences continued. One evening, as Gene sat alone sipping coffee at the kitchen table, he felt the presence of a spirit in the "empty" chair next to him. He pondered the sensation, but quietly finished his midnight snack and went back to bed.

"The next morning as he recounted the incident he was already regretting that he hadn't spoken to the presence. He had been so eager to meet our friend and now, when the opportunity presented itself, he had failed to take advantage of it. Next time, by golly, I'm going to speak to him, he promised himself."

That moment came soon. Mary tells the story: "It was about 8:30 in the evening. As I sat at the kitchen table I gradually became aware of a voice speaking in a low, steady tone. At first I dismissed it, thinking that it was coming from the TV in the living room. But the voice continued. I listened. I could hear the words spoken by the voices on the television, but couldn't distinguish the words of this other voice, only the low tone."

Mary endeavored to listen closer to the mysterious voice. She realized that it was coming from upstairs and that it was her husband's voice. "As I listened," she recalls, "I realized that he was talking to our guest, hoping perhaps to bring him out by talking to him."

When Gene returned downstairs, he related his experiences. He was working upstairs and suddenly felt a cool pressure on the left side of his body. He admitted being startled and nervous but was not frightened. As he worked, he felt the pressure once again. He simply decided to strike up a conversation with his unseen companion.

"Hi! We hope you are happy with us. We're glad you are here and we hope you will stay. We enjoy fixing up this house. We hope you like the way we're fixing it. We would like it if you could give us an indication of the period of time you lived in the house. I wish I knew your name. I hope we can get to a point where we can communicate." A this point, Gene hoped with all his heart, that his verbal message was getting through. And unbeknownst to Gene it was soon to become apparent. that he was, for all intents and purposes, a "medium." He could talk to ghosts!

Gene's attempt at contacting the spirit must have been encouraging. More weird things happened, and Gene and Mary felt they were growing closer to the time that they could communicate openly with whoever was sharing the house with them. They took a new tack — they occasionally asked their unseen friend to give them some kind of sign as to their identity.

One evening they returned home to their empty (?) house and noticed something awry. The clutter of magazines, ashtrays and general livingroom litter was cleared from the coffee table. On the tabletop was one item. Mary writes: "Lying in the center was a five-inch hand-forged spike similar to those we'd found used in the huge tree-beams in the cellar. I wondered where the spike had come from. No sooner had I asked the question than I knew the answer. This was our sign. A hand-made nail. It told so much! Being a part of the house and belonging to the era before machine-cut nails were used extensively, it indicated that our friend had lived in the house when it was first built."

Mary read more into it. She felt the spirit who gave the sign was that of someone who had something to do with the actual building of the house. But she waited to hear Gene's verdict, based on the evidence at hand. "The look on his face told me," Mary said, "that he ws thinking exactly what I was. He held the nail gently between his fingers, rubbing it gently as if he were absorbing the tale it had to tell."

Gene related his interpretation. He felt the spirit was that of an old man who was not the builder, just a friend who helped around the house and was a handyman for the original owners. "Gene held the nail for a long time, examining it and just feeling it as if its touch were putting him in touch with our friend," Mary said.

The couple went to a Berks County powwow doctor for his advice on how to handle their newfound friend. All the powwower offered however, were ways the ghost could be removed from the premises. This was the last thing Gene and Mary wanted to do.

"We were not fearful at any point," Mary continued. "I had moments of apprehension, but Gene, on the other hand, was unnerved by nothing. His openness to whatever might occur made him receptive to experiences that my apprehension closed me to. The appearance of our spirit was something that Gene had longed for almost from the beginning.

"One evening, Gene had gone upstairs to the bathroom. I was in the living room downstairs when I heard him call out a hearty 'Hi there!' It took me a moment to get my bearings: whom was he calling to? But before I could ask, he was calling to me: 'Angel, come up here! I just saw him! I saw our friend!' I ran up the stairs to find Gene coming down the attic stairs his face light with excitement."

The image seemed to float over the stairs leading to the attic. It was smoky gray and the only discernible features of the roughly human-shaped vision was the round face of what Gene described as a pleasant-looking, stocky man in his mid-60s.

When Gene called out to the spirit, it looked at him, smiled and waved slowly. Then, it disappeared up the steps. Gene frantically called for the ghost to stay and talk, but it was too late.

For several weeks following this episode, all was quiet on the ghostly front, and that worried Gene. He was fearful that the wave given by the ghost was a symbol of farewell — a symbol that the spirit was leaving their lives. Gene and Mary had grown quite accustomed to their invisible houseguest. They truly wanted to communicate with it. They were nearly heartbroken with the feeling that the ghost was gone.

Not willing to let the feeling overcome them, they decided almost whimsically to utilize the questionable but oddly reliable services of a Ouija board to seek more information about their friend.

Mary relates their Ouija board experience: "We plunged ahead. 'Can you hear us?' We waited and asked again. 'Can you hear us?' Slowly, haltingly, the tripod began to move, making its way painstakingly toward the "YES" printed at the top, left-hand corner of the board. We looked at each other in disbelief."

Mary and Gene plodded ahead. Slowly, the board unraveled the mysteries. The ghost was present. It was willing to talk, but on its own terms.

"What is your name?"

"Gus."

"Did you go to school?"

"Yes."

"Where?"

"Bernville."

And the adventure continued. Night after night, the board revealed more details until Gene and Mary were able to determine a most remarkable fact. "Gus the Ghost," as Gene and Mary humorously referred to their houseguest, was Gene's great-grandfather!

This changed things a bit.

Quite a bit.

It was when the Ouija board's planchette indicated the family connection that Gene knew he was never to be the same. Deliberately and slowly, Gene and Mary worked the board.

"Gus, do you know anything about my dad?"

"Yes."

"Do you know where he is?"

"Yes . . . he's here."

For many indescribably anxious moments, Gene tried to sort things out. He tried to cope with the proposition that he was able to communicate with spirits, in general, and his dead relatives, in particular. Tears glazed his eyes. He was about to embark on a journey far back within his own life and indeed to generations which preceded him.

Mary continues in her diary: "For several moments Gene was speechless. Then, beneath our fingers the tripod began to move. 'Hello, Gene, this is Dad. It's good to talk to you.' "

Gene was shaken, but the board worked more magic.

"It's all right, Gene, I know how you must feel."

As he regained his composure, Gene joined Mary in another quest.

"Dad, how are you?" The tears continued as Gene built up the courage to communicate to his deceased father.

"I am fine," replied the spirit through the Ouija board.

"Dad, are you happy?"

"Yes, Gene, and I am very proud of you."

At that, Gene broke down. "Angel, I have to stop. My mind is going around in circles!"

The exchange between father and son was so brief, but within it was an enormously powerful force that touched Gene's very soul. And, while the vehicle used to transmit the messages from the other side was, in this case, a Ouija board, the process was to become simplified.

All along, Gene felt that he was sensing the answers to his and Mary's questions before they were confirmed on the board. Sure enough, he continued to examine his own powers and concluded that he was able to communicate with the spirits without the aid of the mystical board.

From that juncture, the lives of all who lived in the house on Pig Hill were altered. Mary abandoned her diary, begun when the events were still unexplained and somewhat of a novelty. Gene reckoned with his talents, abilities, or gifts. The spirits imprisoned for so many years now had a sympathetic voice through which to communicate.

As the facts about the house and its ghostly population unraveled, it was learned that as many as 27 spirits call the place home. From a diary, Mary turned to a written geneological sketch of all of the ghosts. Birth and death dates and other tidbits of information about the lives of those in the spirit world were collected and recorded. The spirits were comfortable with Gene and Mary, and in turn, Gene and Mary were excited about every new discovery.

As the months passed, the ghosts and their mortal mates exchanged conversation and even played practical jokes on each other. Others in Gene and Mary's family were apprised of the situation, and after the initial skepticism passed, all became quite certain that Gene was sincere and really able to communicate with the spirits. In researching this story several independent reports about Gene's powers came to light.

A writer may be tempted to dust off the hackneyed final phrase that may best describe the current situation at Pig Hill — " ... and they all lived happily ever after." But as hackneyed as it may seem, the words are appropriate to this story. The ghosts have been welcomed into Gene and Mary's life, and it is apparent that the ghosts have welcomed Gene and Mary into their existence — wherever and in what form it may be.

EPILOGUE

The stories will never end. As long as man is fascinated by whatever he cannot explain, there will continue to be ghosts and ghost stories.

While mankind may make giant leaps beyond his world, he is pitifully inadequate at understanding his inner world. This world of life, death, and beyond death can be romanticized in fiction and theorized in religion, but somehow only true-to-life experiences, such as many included in this volume, can provide real insight into that mysterious inner world.

The writing of this book has been rewarding and, for the most part, a great deal of fun. There were the tender moments, the sad moments, the moments of fear and coming face-to-face with the ominous powers of the unknown. I have stood atop Witches Hill at midnight, walked over Matthias Schambacher's grave as the rain pelted us on the anniversary of his death. I have walked in the steps of Adeline Baver and Louisa Bissinger — steps which led them to their deaths. I have walked through countless cemeteries in the dead of night, and through abandoned and inhabited houses said to be haunted by ghosts. Still, the quesItion remains: Do ghosts exist?

Only you, the reader, can answer that question. It is an individual matter, answered by each of us in our own way, with our own sources of information and based on our own standards of truth and reality.

There are many more ghost stories out there. I intend to continue to pursue them, and welcome any contributions to this continuing search for the more mysterious side of Berks County's heritage. We live in a county rich in history and legend. But legends are not just stories from the past repeated over and over. Legends begin each and every day, and today's unusual event or unexplainable occurrence or colorful individual could very well become the legend our succeeding generations will be reading about.